"Just as food breaks down to give us a savory experience and fuel us, *Reinventing the Meal* breaks down the art and science of mindful eating to teach us how to enjoy and get what we need from food. It's a guide to using positive life precepts to enrich each and every dining experience from first whiff to final swallow."

— Karen R. Koenig, LCSW, MEd, is the author of four books on eating, including *The Food and Feelings Workbook*

"For years when I've talked to friends about my mindfulness practice, I've paraphrased a line of Thich Nhat Hanh's: 'You can eat the tangerine like this, says the Buddhist monk nonchalantly. Or, he suggests, enunciating with care, you can eat the tangerine like this.' How satisfying to find a whole book that shows me the sublime depth of eating. *Reinventing the Meal* is a mindful pleasure—a dessert from start to finish, and a delicious reminder of the power of awareness."

— Stefanie Marlis, author of *rife, fine, cloudlife*, and other poetry collections

"Pavel Somov brings together mindfulness practices and wisdom from Eastern traditions with scientific insights to thoughtfully challenge and inspire the reader to higher consciousness, all within the arena of the most basic of human activities—eating. He delivers a bounty of food for thought that compellingly assists us in re-imagining ourselves, as well as the meal. In an era of fast-food and fast-paced living, *Reinventing the Meal* offers a well-needed path toward health, serenity, and a meaningful connection to life."

— Jeffrey Weise, PhD, psychologist specializing in the treatment of eating disorders with a private practice in Pittsburgh, PA

Reinventing the Meal

how mindfulness can
help you slow down,
savor the moment &
reconnect with the
ritual of eating

Pavel G. Somov, PhD

New Harbinger Publications, Inc.

Distributed in Canada by Raincoast Books

Copyright © 2012 by Pavel Somov
New Harbinger Publications, Inc.
5674 Shattuck Avenue
Oakland, CA 94609
www.newharbinger.com

Cover design by Amy Shoup
Text design by Michele Waters-Kermes
Acquired by Melissa Kirk
Edited by Jasmine Star

FSC
www.fsc.org
MIX
Paper from
responsible sources
FSC® C011935

Library of Congress Cataloging-in-Publication Data

Somov, Pavel.
  Reinventing the meal : how mindfulness can help you slow down, savor the moment, and reconnect with the ritual of eating / Pavel Somov, PhD ; foreword by Donald Altman, MA, LPC.
      p. cm.
  Summary: "In Reinventing the Meal, renowned psychologist Pavel Somov presents readers with a plan for mindfully reconnecting with the comforting rituals involved in preparing and enjoying food. Chapter by chapter, this guide helps readers reinvent their relationship to food and eventually see each meditative mealtime as an opportunity to reconnect with the body, the mind, and the world at large"-- Provided by publisher.
  Includes bibliographical references.
  ISBN 978-1-60882-101-3 (pbk.) -- ISBN 978-1-60882-102-0 (pdf e-book) (print) -- ISBN 978-1-60882-103-7 (epub) (print)
  1. Food habits--Psychological aspects. 2. Eating (Philosophy) 3. Awareness. I. Title.
TX357.S65 2012
394.1'20019--dc23

                                    2012014107

Printed in the United States of America

14   13   12

10   9   8   7   6   5   4   3   2   1   First printing

To my mother, Irina, who fed my body and taught me love, and to my father, Georgy, who fed my mind and taught me freedom.

Contents

Foreword

The robotic behaviors and fixed mind-sets that drive daily eating habits and mealtime rituals are so deeply ingrained in our lives—personally, psychologically, socially, and culturally—that they often defy attempts to reshape or modify them. How many times, for example, have you heard that it's better not to watch TV and eat at the same time because distraction causes you to eat mindlessly? But did your behavior change?

Here's another example: Do you have certain foods that you tend to eat and others that you avoid? Do you remember the first time you really, *really* tasted something? How about that first grape or the first time you ate a pea? Mentioning those foods now probably brings up a well-established group of thoughts or memories about grapes or peas as something you either "like" or "dislike"—a taste you find "pleasant" or "unpleasant." It's normal that sometime after those first tastes of a new food during childhood, we develop sets of rules or concepts about whether or how to partake of various foods. But if you stopped really tasting most of your food a long time ago, how do you start tasting it again? How do you rediscover eating?

This is the distinct challenge of mindful eating: to break free from entrenched mindless habits and experience things as they really are, including the true sensation of hunger, awareness of flavors, and numerous memories and emotions that arise while you eat, and to be present with each unfolding moment—or morsel, as the case may be. The act of eating can serve as a sacred process that awakens you to all aspects of life and all of the connections that life engenders. Awakening—even a little bit—to the true nature of food, eating, and your own participation in the food chain is no small accomplishment.

As a longtime professional and author in the field of mindful eating, I rarely happen upon writings that so clearly illuminate what is at the core of all mindfulness practice: the awakening of possibility and the possibility of awakening. Pavel Somov has accomplished this in a way that is simultaneously surprising, powerful, fresh, and effective. In *Reinventing the Meal*, he presents a new paradigm for eating by serving up a diverse mindfulness menu consisting of appetizing anecdotes; a savory stew of fascinating scientific research, ancient wisdom, and down-to-earth mindful eating practices; and a delightful dessert of wry humor. In doing so, he stretches the limits of mindful eating, providing approaches that can help people break out of limiting styles of eating and antiquated ways of viewing themselves and the world. No matter how stuck you may feel, this book will metaphorically cleanse your palate, allowing you to start anew—with an empty plate and, more literally, a mind empty of preconceptions about food.

This book offers innovative methods for finding peace with eating, inviting self-reflection, and reconnecting with nature's sacredness. In his quest to reinvent the meal, Pavel conducts a freewheeling exploration that includes such concepts as *oryoki*, a centuries-old Japanese eating meditation, and ahimsa, the Hindu concept of doing no harm, bringing a twenty-first-century slant to these ancient practices. And why not? We greatly need to both embrace and transcend old forms as a means of discovering new forms of expression.

Pavel doesn't sugarcoat the realities of eating, and he refuses to be limited by current concepts. Rather, he takes an imaginative leap and breaks down old models of the meal to concoct a rich new recipe for making food matter again. He asks that instead of opening your mouth, you open your mind. Prepare to be challenged (I know I was!) as *Reinventing the Meal* skillfully leads you into deep self-inquiry and the essence of mindfulness. This is a provocative and courageous book that continually peels away layer after layer from the onion, refusing to settle for easy answers.

As this book attests, your next meal—and the next, and the next—offers an extraordinary opportunity. You are about to embark on a journey that affirms that the fundamental act of living and the light of awakening consciousness are inseparable. Before you venture on, know this: open your mind, and you will never open your mouth in the same way again. And that can only be beneficial.

—Donald Altman
  Author of *One-Minute Mindfulness* and *Meal by Meal*

Escape from Circularity

One of the most interesting early nervous systems is found in the starfish. Here there is a simple ring of nerve cells around the central mouth, with branching nerves into each arm. Since the starfish, physically, can crawl in any direction, it is clear that this nervous system avoids an anarchy of arms when food is available… The mouth-ring tells the muscles, so to speak, where to go and get the food.

— Weston La Barre, *The Human Animal*

My father, who was once a streetwise Russian hooligan and adaptively turned into a prolific Soviet ghostwriter and journalist, while one day pondering something over the kitchen table (his favorite place to write "because the sun's really good here"), remarked out loud, "Nobody *invented* the wheel! It just rolled into our lives all by itself." I remember the moment distinctly. I realized that sometimes things just are what they are. But I was never quite sure of what he had literally meant. Was he referring to the self-referencing propaganda circus of the Soviet life, to the cyclical metamorphosis of "living matter" in this beginningless Universe, or to the hamster wheel of day-to-day routine as we roll—on autopilot—past the treasure trove of timeless moments? Or perhaps he was simply referring to the dazzling, burning wheel of the sun that illuminates our existence.

This pithy image of an uninvited and uninvented eternal wheel stuck with me throughout the years. But back then I was far too young to accept reality in its inexplicable mystery. Come to think of it, I am still existentially young, still running the fool's errand of trying to reinvent every wheel I see. So, thirty or so years since, here I sit at a kitchen table myself (my favorite writing place too, where the sun is almost never good), ready to write an opus about mindful or conscious eating—yet another of many such books in this world—with a promise of nothing less than *reinventing the meal*. The wheel of my mind is spinning still...

While, at a glance, the goal of the book is to awaken the eating zombie, the broader mandate is to explore eating as a platform for meditation and social change. In the pages that follow, I will open the door to reconceptualizing the activity of eating through an eclectic mix of psychology, philosophy, physiology, and spirituality. I will revamp the classic three-course architecture of a meal not just to refocus on the food in front of us but, more importantly, to refocus on the eater. I will endeavor to turn the seeming triviality of a meal into a holistic self-care event. And then—as if totally devoid of all common sense—I will look ahead to the most distant future of human eating, toward the possibility of human photosynthesis. You may call it transhuman nonsense or science fiction, but I will challenge you to dream of a more humane way of being human.

We've been off to a pretty rocky start in this twenty-first century of ours. Ever more enabled to communicate, we have been focusing mostly on our differences. Increasingly overindividualized, we keep losing sight of our sameness. Mindful eating to the rescue! Eating always was and always will be our first and foremost common denominator. As I see it, mindful and conscious eating is perhaps the most effective leverage point for reinfusing meaning and compassion into our shared human project of existence and, possibly, for saving ourselves as a species.

Call me naive, but I believe that global change and peaceful coexistence can emerge from something as simple as a habit of existentially poignant eating. Recognize that in this Universe, which still abides by the second law of thermodynamics and knows no free (energy) lunch, *to eat is to destroy.* How we do it—with grace, moderation, and compassion; or mindlessly, unempathically, and beyond proportion—informs the rest of our living behavior. Will we—like starfish—be guided by our "mouth-rings," or will we, children of the sun, made of stardust, aim toward more enlightened eating? I invite you to toss a monkey wrench into this great wheel of mindless and meaningless eating. I dare you to reinvent the meal!

An Amuse-Bouche of Pattern Interruption

An *amuse-bouche*, which is French for "mouth pleaser," is a miniature preappetizer appetizer. Nothing more than an artistic culinary pirouette and nothing less than a gustatory haiku, an amuse-bouche provokes anticipation and focuses the prospective mind on eating. As such, an amuse-bouche is an attention-focusing device, a priming of the mind, and an elegant mobilization of presence. But most importantly, it is a merciless destroyer of expectations! Indeed, a skillfully executed amuse-bouche explodes preconceived notions and opens the eater's mind to new tasting possibilities. Thus, an amuse-bouche is both a mouth teaser and a mind opener.

In the amuse-bouche sections throughout this book, I invite you to a series of bite-size eating meditations designed to help you empty your mind of preconceived notions about eating before you fill up on new ideas. The goal is nothing less than to clean your mind's palate. I've cooked up nearly seventy of these savory morsels—mind teasers to help you rethink the meaning of eating. Enjoy two or three of these mind teasers daily. They will help you practice opening your mind before you open your mouth.

Eating Is Yoga

The Sanskrit root of the word "yoga" means "to yoke." Therefore, yoga is literally union. In truth, all of your existence is yoga. You are made of this world. You depend on this world. If this world ends—locally or globally—you end too. There is no absolute self-sufficiency, and therefore no stand-alone self. All separation is relative, a trick of the mind. Untrick yourself at your next meal. Recognize that you are not *apart from* this world but *a part of* this world. Eating, just like breathing, reminds you of this union. As such, eating is yoga; eating unifies. And your dinner table is a yoga mat for your mind. Stay in the asana you are in. When you eat, eat.

Eating Earth, Becoming Earth

Everything you are made of has been here all along—oxygen, water, fats, proteins, carbohydrates, enzymes, and endless other molecules and elements. On a fundamental level, you are made of Earth. As you eat, you are eating Earth. As you eat, you are becoming Earth. Made of Earth, you too will be Earth. Earth is eating itself, with gusto, in a kind of self-cannibalism. If this sounds perverse, give it another pass through your mind. It's not as bad as it sounds. Are you familiar with the ourobouros, that ancient symbol of a snake eating its own tail? Eating is one of the cycles of life. The Universe as a whole is studying its own self, chasing its own tail, tasting itself through each self-inquisitive mouthful. So eat to know yourself.

A Stomach Full of Dirt
and Detergents

Everything we eat was once dirt—and arguably still is dirt, just configured beyond recognition. In fact, human digestive enzymes can literally break up dirt, which is why these enzymes are mimicked in some laundry detergents: "to 'eat' the dirt off clothes" (Reader's Digest 2002, 9). Given that we have a stomach full of natural detergents, it's no wonder we're capable of eating mud pies. My point? When I say that we are made of Earth, that we eat Earth, and that we become Earth, I am not being metaphorical. We are literally Earth itself, which is perfectly equipped for self-consumption. Our stomachs full of dirt (food) and detergents (enzymes) are evidence of this eating circularity. The meal-wheel, wherever it goes, travels down a dirt road.

To Eat Is to Know

Eating was the original science, the original study of the environment. Kids, just like primordial life-forms, learn about reality by putting it in their mouths. This mouth knowledge knows no abstracts. The world is either sweet or bitter, smooth or prickly, pleasant or unpleasant. Mouth knowledge comes with gut-level certainty. So to eat is literally to know. But to know what? It is to know self from nonself. Mouth knowledge taught us the boundaries of our bodies. When, as babies, we sucked an object, such as a pacifier, we felt it only from one side, from the side of the mouth. When we sucked our thumbs, we felt them from the outside, through the mouth, and from the inside, through the feeling of the thumb being sucked on. This mouth knowledge—unlike later school knowledge—gave us a glimpse of our paradoxical nature: that somehow we are both the subject and the object of our own experience.

We gave our species the name *Homo sapiens*. That name makes good sense. The word *sapiens* is Latin for both "to know" and "to taste." Yes, we are knowing animals. But do you know what it means to know? To know is to distinguish any given "this" from any given "that." Thus, to know is always dualistic. To know is to sort the one and only reality into "this" and "that." Our most fundamental duality is that of self and other, or ego and eco. As anthropologist Weston La Barre wrote, "An organism's 'knowledge' is its environment" (1954, 3). So to taste is to know. But to taste is also to touch. Touch was the very first evolutionary sense. Living beings knew reality by touching it, that is, by tasting it. We knew self from nonself through eating. So ponder this sapience, wisdom, or knowledge of eating: to eat is to learn.

Body Food Is Mind Food

"Worms are basically blind," wrote William Logan in his book *Dirt: The Ecstatic Skin of the Earth.* "They see by eating... A worm is a long intestine" (1995, 148). A literal living tube, worms track heat/cold and wet/dry polarities and move from the minus of hunger to the plus of fullness by processing the information of the soil by eating it. The worm's body food is its mind food. The same is true of you, dear reader—just on a more sophisticated level. The word "organism" stems from the Greek word *organon*, which means "tool" or "instrument" (a musical organ being an instrument for playing music, and body organs being instruments for specific purposes, such as the liver being an instrument for filtering blood). Thus the body is an instrument for processing information, whether that means reading this sentence (mind food) or biting into an apple (body food). Eating is knowing. Got mind food? If not, chew on.

Wise Dirt, Humble Soil, Knowing Earth

Homo sapiens—how beautifully and wisely we have named ourselves. Our first (genus) name, *Homo*, has its roots in the soil. The word "homo" is related to the words "humus," "humble," and "humility," all of which mean "dirt" or "earth." Our last (species) name, *sapiens*, takes its origin from the Latin verb *sapere*, which has two meanings: "to know" and "to taste." So here we are: Wise Dirt, Humble Soil, Knowing Earth. As you sit down for another meal, recall that you are Earth, that you are eating Earth, that you are becoming Earth as you eat this Earth. Partake with sapience, with humility, and with self-knowledge.

Time for a Tail Wag, Fish!

Did you know that not all that long ago, you (yes, you!) had a tail? I'm not talking about evolution; I'm talking your very own embryonic history. At about four and half weeks' gestation, when you still didn't know air and lived like a fish inside the liquid medium within your mother's amniotic sac, you had a large, tadpolelike head and a tail and resembled "a prehistoric animal" (Nilsson 1990, 80). So let me ask you: What would have been different about your eating choices, "human," if you hadn't lost your tail? Time for a mindful tail wag, human fish!

No One Eats Alone

Eating is a communal endeavor. Even those who are doing solitary time don't eat alone. When you eat, you are assisted by a myriad of friendly bacteria. Much of your digestion is literally outsourced to the legions of digestive foot soldiers that live, toil, and die within you to help you live. Take a moment to acknowledge the unseen mouths that are helping you digest the food you eat.

You Are Feeding a World

When you eat, you aren't feeding yourself alone. You are host to countless lives. Trillions upon trillions of microbes, mites, and even parasites live inside you and depend entirely upon you for their sustenance. When you eat, you are participating in an economy that feeds an entire microcosm. You are an ecology—in a manner of speaking, a ground of being for trillions of invisible lives that you sustain while feeding yourself. You are a mini Earth, a biosphere, a fertile soil for all of the beings that grow in and on you. When you sit down for your next meal, recognize that you are feeding a world that is both you and not you at the same time. Ponder this paradox of existence.

Share your mindful eating experiences online using the Mindful Eating Tracker at http://www.eatingthemoment.com/mindfulness-tracker.

chapter 1

When the Meal-Wheel Rolled In

Mankind when created did not know of bread for eating or garments for wearing. The people walked with limbs on the ground, they ate herbs with their mouths like sheep, they drank ditch-water.

— Ancient Sumerian hymn

No one invented eating. Eating—as a form of metabolic dependence on the environment—is as old as life. As paleontologist Richard Fortey notes in his book *Life: A Natural History of the First Four Billion Years of Life on Earth*, "Life is a thief." Indeed, "to feed its growth, an energy-yielding reaction is stolen by the living cell" (1998, 41). Thus, to live *is* to eat, meaning to consume—that is, to take from the environment, from others. Life, to paraphrase Fortey, is fundamentally self-serving: it views its environment as a serving of food. The evolution of living is synonymous with the evolution of eating.

Eating a meal, however, is an entirely different matter. While no one invented eating per se, the social institution of a meal has clear-cut historical footprints. Meal-based eating was born of human attempts to optimize the food supply, and specifically born of the enterprise of agriculture.

The Birth of Centralized Eating

We didn't always have meals. Less than three hundred generations ago we were still hunter-gatherers. Eating was individualized. We ate only as much as we were motivated (by hunger) to gather and kill. We fasted and feasted. We lived off the bush. We were largely at the mercy of Mother Nature. We didn't worry, however; we still had that primordial Zen. We trusted the Mother. But then roughly ten thousand years ago in Sumeria, on "the great alluvial plain from the site of the modern city of Baghdad, where the [rivers] Tigris and...Euphrates approach most closely to each other," we panicked and invented agriculture (Woolley 1965, 1).

Why? We grew weary and wary of being dependent on nature. We felt worried that Mother Nature would fail us and we would go without. We yearned for certainty of food supply. We wanted to guarantee our survival. This was, arguably, a culturally neurotic turn of events. We decided to try to control our own fate by controlling our food supply. We started planning and planting, accounting and rationing. Math was born, as were the pragmatics of social engineering, including such notions as time (to coordinate human activity) and measurement (to assure justice, fairness, equality, and accountability). The birth of agriculture was the end of individualized eating. The meal was born! But in planting the seeds of future civilizations, we also planted the seeds of modern-day mindless eating.

The Birth of Mindless Eating

Agriculture led to surpluses of food. But instead of celebrating our good fortune in eating, we started to take food for granted. Once the sole goal of our daily behavior, eating started to become a routine. And instead of rejoicing in the simple triumph of surfeit, we started to merge eating with entertainment. Mindless eating was born. The activity of eating, which was once a hunger-timed, stomach-specific, person-specific event, became a generic, time-based activity, subject to the demands of our collective existence.

When we live by ourselves, we are forced to be self-sufficient—each Jane is a jack-of-all-trades, and each mind minds its own business. When we group, we begin to specialize: some hunt, some gather, some plant, some harvest, some prepare food, some trade it, some govern, and some do nothing. Collective living leads to coordination of activity, organization, and centralization. This takes us away from our individual needs and idiosyncratic rhythms and puts us on a schedule. We start to program each other, coming up with rules and traditions and enforcing them. Eventually, we turn into habit-powered, mindless automatons. We start to operate on time, eating when it's "time to eat," rather than when we feel hungry enough to eat. We start to lose touch with reality and ourselves. In this way, agriculture—which demands a rule-bound civilization—turned us into zombies. Mindful, conscious eating is, therefore, psychologically libertarian eating. It is a return to self.

The Birth of Overeating

Because collective living led to division of labor, it in turn led to social inequalities, which in turn led to differential access to food, which in turn led to eating in accordance with social status rather than one's metabolic needs. That's right: once on the road, the meal-wheel of mindless eating just kept on turning. Those with the means ate more than they needed. Those without the means ate less than those with the means, but generally still more than was typical during hunter-gatherer days. In addition, village life, with its surpluses of food, meant sedentary life (Schick and Toth 1993), and therefore a reduced need for consumption. Overeating was born.

The Birth of Mass Overeating

There is no agriculture without math. Yet wherever there's centralization and math, there's also a promise of math-based objectivity and thus a monopoly on truth, eventually leading to social inequality. Wherever there is social inequality, there's inequality in access to food, and thus social unrest. And wherever a society swings out of control in this way, there is a need for politics, particularly the politics of appeasement with food—for example, the Roman dictum of giving the masses food and entertainment, preferably combined. Food procurement, which was once a strictly personal undertaking, became subject to social control. In trying to control Mother Nature, we ended up controlling each other and eating out of control, due to the cheap, low-quality politics of appeasement with food. Over the millennia, the industrial-agricultural elites finally figured out how to provide masses with cheap, low-quality food, and in the process, mass overeating was born.

The Birth of Decorative Eating

According to a somewhat smug ancient Sumerian hymn, "Mankind when created did not know of bread for eating or garments for wearing" (Woolley 1965, 13). But even when our species didn't know of bread, it certainly knew how to enjoy eating. Unfortunately, we—the well fed, well dressed, and civilized—forgot all about this basic ecstasy of living. We grew bored with food. We started to dress food up, and we started to dress up to eat. This birth of decorative eating was and is born of our ongoing desperation to connect with reality. Our ceaseless pursuit of culinary stimulation is, at root, a craving for nature. We hunger for a sense of raw vibrancy, but we keep looking for it in ever-more-processed and ever-more-decorated foods. We have forgotten that hunger and mindfulness are still the best chefs in town, capable of turning any reasonably palatable morsel of food into a foodgasm.

The Birth of Unempathic Eating

There's a Russian phrase that refers to those who invent stimulation because of having too much: *s zhiry besishsya*, meaning "gone fat crazy." This makes sense. Back in the evolutionary day, having a layer of adipose tissue provided us with a bit of portable food reserve. Excess was a good thing. But now that most of us sport a size or two worth of this adipose clothing, we are ever on the lookout for something novel, something thrilling. However, we haven't been all that creative. Roller coasters aside, most of us seem to keep looking for stimulation in food, just like the ancients. Mark Kurlansky, in describing the eating practices of the Roman elite, wrote, "Patricians ate an elaborate cuisine that expressed opulence in ingredients and presentation. Roman cooks seemed to avoid leaving anything in its natural state. They loved the esoteric, such as sow's vulva and teats, a dish…which provoked a debate as to whether it should be from a virgin sow or…one whose first litter was aborted" (2002, 61).

Modern-day eaters are similarly ever in search of something more exotic. It is only natural: thanks to large-scale industrial agriculture, we have totally lost touch with nature. However, being hunter-gatherers at heart, we are jonesing for a taste of something wild and natural. But unlike our hunter-gatherer predecessors, we lack a sense of humble tact and grace as we take from Mother Nature. This lack of awareness knows no dietary bounds. When I mindlessly down a glass of carrot juice, ignorant of the original life behind it—the plant life that has been "freshly squeezed" out of existence—am I not just as out of touch with Mother Nature as an oblivious omnivore?

Life is life, whether you can relate to it or not, whether it silently meets the impersonal blade of a combine during harvest or squeals like a butchered pig, whether it falls from the sky when shot dead in midair or breathlessly thrashes in your hands with a hook through its cheek. Animals, plants, insects, and even the good bacteria that we swallow by the millions with each spoonful of yogurt—whatever we eat and consume—all of this is but different manifestations of the same life that flows through us. All of this *is* us.

It's an axiom of living: we don't eat rocks; we eat life. And when we do so mindlessly, we eat without grace, without empathy, without compassion. Before large-scale agriculture, we were too close to life to not notice it. Naturally, we felt grateful. But now, barricaded behind shelves of denatured, processed, packaged foods, we don't see the life that we ingest.

Going back to our hunter-gatherer roots is, of course, a naively romantic and implausible proposition, given our social evolution. We are what we are: *information* hunter-gatherers. We are way past living off the bush. Indeed, we're on the brink of self-guided, technologically assisted genetic mutations. So wave a fond good-bye to a preagricultural way of living. We missed that train. It vanished in the mystery of our wild origins. And that's fine. There are other ways to wake up from this dream of mindless and ungrateful eating. There is still plenty of time to regain our primordial sense of humble appreciation for the life that we take in order to sustain ourselves, until we find a better, less zero-sum path of existence.

The Meal-Wheel Runaround

The Sumerian "apostles of civilization" (Woolley 1965, 13) who invented agriculture and time-based, centralized, institutionalized eating, those smug social engineers who ridiculed precivilized humans as not knowing bread and as drinking ditch-water, were soon to run into an ongoing sequence of ironies. Agriculture, with its promise of an assured food supply, paradoxically led to food shortages and malnourishment. Agricultural settlements ate a far less diverse diet than their hunter-gatherer predecessors (Jones 1993). In addition, Mother Nature was objectified. The primordial relationship with land started to shift from an attitude of graceful gratitude to one of production and commercialization. The more we, as a civilization, wanted to be in control, the more we wanted and the more we took. The more we took, the less there was for the land to give us. So we hit the road in search of more land to cultivate. But monoculture was a lousy solution, and implementing it in new locales didn't make it any better. Eventually, when we essentially ran out of new lands to cultivate, we resorted to ever-more-myopic agricultural and agronomic technologies to leverage more out of the land. This meal-wheel of centralized food production and consumption has circled the world and failed in every land. The end result? We are undernourished yet overweight.

What about the Ditch-Water Drinkers Who Know No Bread?

So how have the few remaining hunter-gatherer cultures fared in the meantime? Consider the Hadza people of northern Tanzania, whose genetic makeup "indicates that they may represent one of the primary roots of the human family tree—perhaps more than 100,000 years old" (Finkel 2009, 104). The Hadza raise no crops or livestock; they work part-time and live full-time, enjoying "an extraordinary amount of leisure time" (104) and living "a remarkably present-tense existence" (112). To call their subsistence activities "work" is really a misnomer. This "work," with its hunter's hyperfocus and its gatherer's attunement to environment, easily doubles as meditation—and triples as exercise. Of particular pertinence is the fact that the Hadza "have no known history of famine" (104) and are nutritionally better fed than their "civilized" counterparts. "The Hadza diet remains even today more stable and varied than that of most of the world's citizens" (104). Unlike more "advanced" cultures with their progressively more esoteric tastes and ways of cooking, ranging from those Roman cooks who "seemed to avoid leaving anything in its natural state" (Kurlansky 2002, 61) to modern-day molecular gastronomists, the Hadza cooking style is simple: "No grill. No pan" (Finkel 2009, 115).

While complexity might serve as an index of a civilization's age, simplicity is an index of its wisdom. I'm not saying you should stop eating bread and should drink water from a ditch, but I am saying that it's time to examine our fundamental assumptions about eating in general, and meal-based, institutionalized eating in particular. Let's shrug off that Sumerian sense of superiority, with its centralized, schedule-driven eating. And let's go one step further and do the truly civilized thing: let's open our minds.

Conclusion: A Fix-a-Flat for the Meal-Wheel

The meal-wheel has been rolling around for quite a while, and it's obviously here to stay. However, it's sorely in need of a retreading job. In 1987, Jared Diamond, a UCLA professor of geography and physiology, declared that the invention of agriculture was humanity's "biggest mistake" (1987, 64). I disagree. Agriculture was no mistake.

Centralization was no mistake. Math was no mistake. Social engineering was no mistake. All of these inventions of the human mind were a psychological necessity. They logically flow from our very nature. We—the human animals, the modern-day apes—are irrevocably far more neurotic than our evolutionary predecessors. We sport massive brains. We are full of nerves, literally and metaphorically. We are a highly innervated, densely wired, touchy, sensitive species. Neural geniuses, we are fiercely creative and subject to chronic angst. Our minds are double-edged swords that both keep us worried and prompt us to proactively solve problems.

Our minds are of the nature of the wheel: We keep rolling from a thought to a thought to a thought, traveling down well-trodden neural paths and taking occasional detours triggered by the creativity of our panic. We program ourselves, deprogram ourselves, and reprogram ourselves, and then do all of this over and over again. That's our paradox—the dialectic of human nature. I am not opposed to it. I celebrate it. I am in awe of it.

The meal-wheel *had* to be invented. We were simply too smart, too observant not to invent it. As we watched the great wheel-like pattern of nature, a combination of hunger and wonderment spurred us to develop hypotheses about controlling the food supply and then put them to the test. As agriculture evolved, we organized, centralized, and institutionalized ourselves and our sustenance. We turned ourselves into eating zombies. This was our neurotic best. Now it's time to correct the course of our eating evolution. It's time to decentralize, deinstitutionalize, recustomize, and repersonalize our eating—time to recalibrate eating to our moment-to-moment needs. It's time to unhitch eating from the mental abstraction of time and hitch it back to the sensory immediacy of the body. It's time to rediscover the timelessness of eating and reinflate this flat meal-wheel, now empty of meaning, with a fresh breath of presence. It's time to get back on course.

An Amuse-Bouche of Pattern Interruption

I hope you have saved some room in your mind for another serving of pattern interruption. As you sit down for your next meal, take a moment to read through one of the eating meditations that follow. Let these strange and provocative ideas about eating open your mind. And then, with your mind open, open your mouth. So, pull up your chair and tuck in your napkin: it's time to rethink who is eating.

Brain Food

Sea squirts have a tubular shape like a worm. Physician, psychiatrist, and clinical researcher Stuart Brown describes them intriguingly (2009, 47–48):

> The sea squirt is one of our most ancient relatives. Its primitive nervous system makes it more closely related to humans than the sponges and corals it resembles. Scientists say a sea squirt tadpole approximates what an early human ancestor—the very first chordate—may have looked like some 550 million years ago. In this larval form, it has a primitive spinal cord and bundle of ganglia that act as a functional brain. This tiny brain helps it move selectively toward nutrients and away from harm… Once the sea squirt grows to adulthood, it attaches itself permanently to a rock or a boat's hull or pilings. It no longer needs to monitor the world as it did as a juvenile because the passing current provides enough nutrients for it to survive…

The adult sea squirt becomes the couch potato of the sea. In a surprisingly macabre twist, the sea squirt digests its own brain. Without a need to explore or find its sustenance, the creature devours its own cerebral ganglia.

Two questions to ponder before your next meal: What is the point of the digestive system? And what is the point of the brain?

We Are Tubes

One Russian word for "living" is *zhivoi*. A Russian for "stomach" is *zhivot*. See any fundamental difference? I don't. To eat is to live and to live is to eat. We are tubes—conscious, even spiritual, but nevertheless digestive tubes that metabolize the environment, through a one-way transaction, to keep on living. From an evolutionary standpoint, the brain (including the one reading this sentence) came along after the emergence of the stomach. The point of the brain is to fill the tube of life with food so it can go on living, and to navigate this tube toward greener pastures and away from becoming someone else's lunch. This isn't reductionism. It's just a point of view for you to entertain before you stuff your own digestive tube at your next meal.

Snakes on Legs

Peristalsis is a wave of muscular contraction and relaxation that moves food onward through your digestive track. This mechanism isn't just found inside the human gut. Snakes, for example, use peristalsis to swallow prey whole. If you've seen pictures of the twenty or so feet of coiling loops of the human small intestine, and if you bear in mind the peristaltic waves of contraction and relaxation that propel food through your gut, and if you understand that, like all humans, you have a reptilian brain structure inside your skull, then you will have no problem imagining yourself as a snake on legs. And after all, what is a snake if not a living, breathing, feeling, thinking, decision-making tube? Ponder this as you worm your way into yet another pile of food.

Metabolically Adrift

Various species of *Riftia* tube worms are among the most abundant animals inhabiting the areas in close proximity to deep-sea vents. According to professor of zoology Rob Dunn, they have "no mouths, anus, or digestive tract" (2009, 177). So how do these creatures nourish themselves? They don't—at least not actively. Instead, they have a trophosome, an organ that houses microbes. In exchange for this fertile place to reproduce, the microbes provide the tube worms with nutrients. Dunn said, "The tube worms are not unlike trees… [They] use their long gills like leaves to harness the energy around them" (177–178). That's one take. Another is captured in the name itself: these creatures are literally living tubes, metabolically adrift. My point? We aren't all that different. Humans are also living tubes, though we're a tad more complicated. Just because our digestive tube has a mouth and is attached to the GPS of our CNS (central nervous system), along with the musculoskeletal apparatus that provides protection and means of locomotion, it doesn't mean we aren't living tubes. We are. But instead of staying in one place and sifting our surrounding for nutrients, we walk the road of life from a meal to a meal to a meal.

Why does it matter? Because it matters what matter flows through us. And because it matters how we pass through this matter—consciously or unconsciously. To eat is to pass through the environment and let the environment pass through you. So my question to you is: Are you metabolically and experientially adrift? Are you metabolically plowing through random food environments without paying any mind to what you're plowing through? Are you mindlessly and indiscriminately drilling your way through years of food? What is passing through you, living tube? What are you passing past, living tube?

Something to Absorb

Life is inside; environment is outside. Eating is a process of consuming the environment. When we eat, we absorb the outside world into our inner world. Consider tapeworms. Just like the *Riftia* (the tube worms described above), tapeworms have no intestine, so, in the words of visionary filmmaker John Downer, "they absorb food directly from the liquids that flow over them... [Thus], their outer surface is effectively their stomach lining" (1991, 177). That may sound strange, but is it really? Don't we humans also absorb various substances through the skin? Of course we do. If we didn't, topical medicines and ointments wouldn't exist. So take a look at your face in the mirror and consider that the skin you see is another manifestation of your stomach. An interesting idea to absorb, isn't it?

The Great Wheel of Appetite

The Sanskrit word *samsara* refers to the Buddhist and Hindu concept of the wheel of suffering. Evolutionary technicalities aside, as animals we are essentially plants with brains and means of locomotion. Indeed, flora and fauna are simply two different platforms of living: sedentary and mobile. Plants stay put; they are wherever they are. Each blade of grass is a Buddhist monk of sorts, rooted and grounded in Earth.

Animals, on the other hand, humans included, are in a constant state of search. We want, we fantasize, we dream, we yearn, we chase, we pursue, and we suffer. I like to think of us as "walking trees" because we are physically and mentally mobile, ever on the go and caught up in the samsaric wheel of appetite. We always want more than what is given. We evolved to pursue, so we pursue. A wheel of desire, we endlessly roll along, physiologically restless, existentially fidgety, constantly craving this or that.

And just like a wheel creates motion, the wheel of psychophysiological appetite creates a continuous *e-motion* of dissatisfaction ("e-motion" for endogenous—that is, internal—motion). The wheel of the human body-mind knows no contentment unless it stops, and it is fullness that stops the wheel, if only for a fleeting moment. When we finally feel satisfied, we can finally slow down, pause, and rest—but not for long. After all, it is the nature of a wheel to roll. So before long, the wheel of appetite revs up the engine of restlessness.

If fullness, however transient, is the destination, eating is the restless journey. The next time you sit down to a meal, notice the excavating movements of your hands, drawing reality into you as you eat. Experience yourself as a wheel of appetite in search of a pause. Next time you feel full, recognize that you—the walking tree—have once again arrived at a fleeting moment of contentment. Notice the moment of satisfaction and rest your hands. Veg out, mind-wheel, veg out—just like your plant kin. Allow yourself to enjoy these fleeting moments of fullness when the wheel of your hunger finally has nowhere to go. Allow yourself to cease the restless locomotion of eating. Let the samsara wheel of your appetite come to a brief pause. Enjoy the rest stop on this road of desire.

Share your mindful eating experiences online using the Mindful Eating Tracker at http://www.eatingthemoment.com/mindfulness-tracker.

chapter 2

First Course: Reconnecting with Your Body

Breath is our primary food.

> — Lorin Roche, *Breath Taking*

An old-school meal is food-centered and typically consists of three food-centered courses, such as an appetizer (a soup or a salad), a main course, and a dessert. In the paradigm I propose—the new meal— eating is both food-centered and eater-centered and also consists of three courses, but the focus is on activities:

1. A course of relaxation in which you reconnect with your body (the topic of this chapter)

2. A course of mindfulness in which you reconnect with your mind (chapter 3)

3. A course of mindful eating in which you reconnect with your world through food (chapter 4)

The goal of the new meal paradigm is to change our modern-day routine of mindless eating into a daily program of total body-mind self-care. Starting your meals with a course of relaxation is the first vital step.

Restoring the Flow of Well-Being

In the old paradigm of the meal, the word "course" refers to food. In the new paradigm the word "course" refers to an activity of self-care. It is of note that the word "course" has its origin in the Latin word *cursus*, which means "onward movement" and includes the flow, or course, of a river. The new meal courses in this book are designed to restore the flow of well-being. Recall that we are essentially very smart digestive tubes on legs. Evolutionarily, nervous systems and the capacity for loco-motion set the original vector of well-being: from nonfood (hunger or emptiness, which is an existential minus) to food (fullness or satisfaction, which is an existential plus). The new meal paradigm is designed to synchronize the currents of your body and mind into one harmonious flow of metabolic and psychospiritual self-renewal. The idea is to get your techno-distracted monkey mind back on course (no offense, modern ape). In sum, the new meal paradigm is the yoga of eating.

Relaxation: A Logical Place to Start

Whereas an old-school meal begins with turning on the TV and zoning out, the new meal is a total body-mind self-care event that begins with a first course of conscious and relaxing intake of air and water. There are several good reasons for using relaxation as the first course, and we'll look at them in detail below:

- Relaxation is restorative, grounding, and centering.

- It facilitates digestion.

- It aids in stress management to help prevent emotional overeating.

- It primes the sense of smell, which leverages maximum enjoyment and facilitates fullness.

- Preloading with smell and flavor prior to eating facilitates satiety, or fullness.

- Breath-focused relaxation can help promote awareness of fullness, which helps prevent overeating.

- Relaxation provides a reality check through the rediscovery of your physical or bodily dimension.

Follow the Survival Priorities

At a minimum, human life requires air, water, and food. Everything else is extra. It makes sense to start with the physiological basics: air and water. After all, we can go without food for quite some time. For example, in 2006 a Russian-Armenian man, Agasi Vartanyan, went without food for fifty days straight (Associated Press 2006). If this sounds impressive, consider some of the record holders for fasting in the animal kingdom. A python can go for a year and half without eating. The African lungfish (which sports both gills and lungs) can slow down its metabolism enough to survive without any food whatsoever for two years. The Australian burrowing frog can live without food for a whopping five years. And the microscopic creatures known as tardigrades can go without food for an amazing eight years (*Science Illustrated* 2010).

The point is, food can wait. It's a bit different with water. The timeline for terminal dehydration is person-specific, but it may occur as quickly as in three days. As for oxygen deprivation, yogic and free-diving training aside, most of us would peter out without air after three minutes. So the intake priorities are clear: air, then water, then food. Therefore the new meal begins with conscious and mindful intake of air and water. The sequence is easy to remember: just follow the survival priorities.

A Sky Full of Food

According to the Atharvaveda, an ancient Hindu text, "The breathing in and the breathing out are rice and barley" (Zaehner 1966, 28). Indeed, look up or look out the window to notice this amazing sky full of our primary fuel—now, not later. Go ahead and put the reading aside for a moment and take a look at this atmospheric placenta that nourishes our earthly existence. Recognize that, unlike food, air is still free and needs no cooking. Cultivate a habit of starting your meals with mindful belly breaths to prevent any future bellyaches from mindless overeating. Have yourself a snack of lungfuls!

The Best-Kept Relaxation Secret

If I were to ask, "When is the best time to relax?" you'd probably say, "When you're feeling stressed." True, that would be the best time to intervene with relaxation. But when is the best time to utilize relaxation in all its calming potency? The answer might surprise you: right before you eat. You see, the classic yoga technique of abdominal or diaphragmatic breathing, known as *pranayama*, works best when you have maximum diaphragmatic control, and that occurs when your stomach is empty. Patanjali, an ancient yogi who "codified" the subtleties of *pranayama*, noted the importance of practicing *pranayama* prior to meals. I'm sure you've noticed how sometimes you feel short of breath after overeating, and maybe even how your breathing becomes a bit labored after eating just a moderate amount.

Some of this is purely mechanical. The distention of the stomach competes with the working of the diaphragm, a horizontal muscle located between the chest cavity and the stomach cavity. But some of it is biochemical. Soviet physician-scientist Konstantin Pavlovich Buteyko, a student of breath and yoga now renowned for his asthma control method, explains that digestion of food by the body's cells is a kind of "inner breathing" that has the effect of intensifying the overall respiration rate of the organism, leading to hyperventilation and shortness of breath, and that this occurs after eating moderately, let alone after overeating (Buteyko 1977).

So just like you wouldn't go swimming on a full stomach, it doesn't make sense to practice diaphragmatic breathing on a full or even half-full stomach. Sure, any relaxation is better than nothing, but why not take advantage of the perfect window of opportunity for relaxation, which happens to be right before the meal? This timing, then, is the best-kept secret of relaxation training. A couple of times a day, when your stomach is almost completely empty, you are perfectly positioned to tap the maximum relaxation benefits from practicing some simple relaxation steps for a few minutes.

In addition to providing a dose of restorative relaxation, performing a brief abdominal breathing exercise two or three times a day before you eat is a great way to develop a well-timed stress management routine. After all, while we may struggle to set aside time for stress management, we hardly ever forget to eat. One way or another, we find time for nutritional self-maintenance on a daily basis. So anchoring your relaxation to the basic self-maintenance behavior of eating assures that you won't forget to remember to relax.

Allow yourself to begin to think of eating as relaxation and of relaxation as the first course of every meal. Fundamentally, both air intake and food intake are metabolic import-export activities. Each new breath, just like each new bite, forces out waste products. Ponder this miraculous circularity: to exhale, you have to inhale, and to vacate your bowels you have to fill them (no intake means no peristalsis, which means no bowel movement).

Inaugurate the New Routine

Any project of change begins with a first step. Sometimes the first step is huge: you drive across town and plunk down five grand on a hot tub. But sometimes the first step is very small: you go get a screwdriver. The first step that I propose is of the latter kind—small, easy, effortless. Starting with your very next meal, have some air for your first course. Shortly I'll give you some specific breath-focused relaxation practices, but for now simply begin your meal with a moment of conscious breathing. Let this small step inaugurate your new meal routine.

If you have only enough patience for one mindful breath, so be it—for now. The amount of air you consciously serve yourself doesn't matter at this point, nor does the technique you use. What does matter is that you start cultivating a habit of filling up on air right before you eat. Wherever you are in time, there is a meal looming on your horizon—maybe in a minute, maybe in a few hours, maybe tomorrow morning. Start your next meal with wide-open lungs, and remind yourself: first a lungful, then a mindful, and only then a mouthful. Reconnect with your body through breath, then reconnect with yourself through a moment of mindful self-awareness (which I'll discuss in chapter 3), and then—and only then—reconnect with the world at large through mindful, conscious eating (more about this in chapter 4).

Turbocharge Your Relaxation Response

As a past owner of a couple of turbocharged cars, I can personally attest to the triumph of turbo acceleration! It's the mechanical equivalent of a power breath. It compresses the ambient air and delivers it to the air intake manifold at higher than normal pressure, increasing power and torque. In a very real sense, turbo is a deep breath.

But whereas the mechanical turbo is all about the in-breath, the turbo of relaxation is about the out-breath. Contrary to the oft-heard advice to take a deep breath, the true payoff of relaxation actually comes from exhalation, not inhalation. As neuroscientist and Zen practitioner James Austin explains, "Breathing *out* quiets down the activity of many nerve cells. Expiration slows the firing of nerve cells in the amygdala... Such slowings, taking place in the limbic system and elsewhere, may contribute to the basic calming effect" (1999, 461–462). According to Austin, chanting and focusing on the breath both "increase the inhibitory tone of the vagus nerves" (94), which correlates with the experience of relaxation.

Thus, inspiration (inhaling) activates and expiration (exhaling) relaxes. Take a deep breath and your pupils will dilate, as they would if you were afraid or excited. Exhale and your pupils will constrict slightly. This is worth committing to memory: relaxation is enhanced by spending more time breathing out. So to turbocharge your relaxation, prolong the out-breath. One way to pace the out-breath is by counting (to four, for example). But personally, I find this kind of breath arithmetic a bit annoying. In my opinion, chanting or humming is far more intuitive. (I'll discuss the specifics of that in a moment.)

Another way to slow the out-breath is by breathing through the nose, which also appears to play a role in facilitating relaxation. As Austin explains, "The flow of air along the nasal passages also influences the brain, because air flow stimulates nasal nerve endings. These stimuli go on to induce a rhythmical 40 CPS [cycles per second] activity up in the olfactory bulb, which is the higher extension of the central nervous system overlying the nasal passages" (1999, 95).

This notion that merely prolonging the exhalation and breathing quietly through the nose allows us to downregulate the central nervous system means that abdominal breathing through the nose with a prolonged exhalation phase is a kind of brake pedal that serves as a relaxation accelerator. So… Ready, set, exhale! Ahh…

Try This: Extend the Out-Breath

A natural way to prolong the exhalation phase is to either breathe out through pursed lips or hum as you exhale. Here's an easy way to compare these techniques to simply exhaling through your nose: After taking a deep in-breath through your nose, exhale through your nose and try to prolong the out-breath. Then take another deep breath and hum quietly as you exhale. Notice how humming out the air easily and effortlessly extends the out-breath. Finally, take a deep breath and exhale through pursed lips. The difference between the latter two and just breathing out through your nose is probably quite obvious, but you could try timing all three types of exhalation to compare how long they last.

Here's a tip: Cleanse your nasal passages first, either by blowing your nose or by using a neti pot (a device for rinsing the nasal passages that has its origins in ayurvedic medicine). Having your nose clean enough to hum will also allow you to savor the aroma of food more fully.

Nitric Oxide: The Best-Kept Secret of Humming

Hum out a few breaths. Notice the sound. Now fake a foodgasm, moaning out an "mmm" of appreciation. Notice the sound. Humming and mmm-ing sound the same, don't they? This little curiosity is another well-kept secret, and it has a bearing on relaxation. Nasal humming (and chanting, for that matter) triggers the release of a substantial amount of nitric oxide (NO). What's the significance of this? Louis Ignarro, distinguished professor of pharmacology at the UCLA School of Medicine and a 1998 Nobel Prize laureate for his discovery of the importance of nitric oxide, describes NO as "the body's natural cardiovascular wonder drug" (2005, xiii).

According to a report in the *American Journal of Respiratory and Critical Care Medicine*, "The paranasal sinuses are major producers of nitric oxide (NO)." The researchers hypothesized that "oscillating airflow produced by humming would enhance sinus ventilation and thereby increase nasal NO levels" (Weitzberg and Lundberg 2002, 144). Indeed, their study found that humming increased nasal NO by a factor of fifteen when compared to quiet exhalation.

Why is this of any relevance to the first course of the new meal? Because nitric oxide release happens to both accompany and power up the relaxation effect. Here's what the godfather of Western relaxation research, Herbert Benson, MD, had to say about nitric oxide in his book *Relaxation Revolution*: "Those practicing mind body techniques [tend] to experience lower blood pressure, calmer brain activity, *healthful emissions of nitric oxide in the body's cells*, and other physical and emotional benefits" (Benson and Proctor 2010, 22, my italics). Benson explains that "release of nitric oxide in the body's cells...serves as a vasodilator, an agent that expands blood vessels. This dilation process can be highly effective in reducing blood pressure" (129). He also explains that nitric oxide is "associated with good health, including antibacterial and antiviral responses and also beneficial changes in the cardiovascular system" (77).

This curious tidbit of psychophysiology is a gem of mindful eating know-how. Eventually I'll help you incorporate this relaxing effect of nasal humming into the architecture of the new meal. But first I'll present a couple of awareness-building exercises.

Try This: Make "Mmm" Your Mantra

Consider "mmm" as a mantra of gustatory enjoyment—the om of mindful eating. "Mmm" is the music of savoring. And indeed, this sound, like no other, celebrates the awareness of pleasure. We mmm-oan during an orgasm or intense pleasure. We mmm-oan during pain in self-soothing. We mmm-oan in appreciation of flavor. Practice amplifying your eating experience by making the "mmm" sound as you slow down to savor a particularly felicitous eating moment. But also get in a habit of mmm-ing in anticipation of the first bite.

Try This: Have Some Noms

Let's try a bit of semantic magic. Consider the following mnemonic equation:

$$NO \text{ (nitric oxide)} + OM \text{ (mantra)} = NOM$$

Voilà! What used to be a slang word for eating with pleasure has been transformed into an easy-to-remember mnemonic for relaxation as the first course. How does it work? Simple: before you eat (with conscious and mindful pleasure) make some nom sounds. Go ahead and try out this sound of satisfaction to appreciate its hum-ful, soothing nasality. Have yourself some satisfying noms of relaxation *before* you eat.

Try This: Hum Along

Recently I had a chance to attend a reunion of the Das Brothers, Krishna Das and Lama Surya Das. At some point the two sat on the stage as Krishna Das led an audience of two hundred or so people in an hour-long chant of Hindu mantras. Not knowing most of these syllables, let alone their meanings, many of the folks in the audience seemed to just hum along. The resultant effect was a choir of soothing, flowing vibration. When Krishna Das breathed out his final chant, there wasn't a single sound of applause; no one made a noise for what seemed like at least two minutes. Judging by my own experience, the crowd simply had melted into their seats in profound relaxation. Krishna Das wisely allowed us to take our time to collect ourselves, and then we reunited in another, far more Western sound: the percussive clapping of ovation.

My point is this: humming and chanting are powerfully relaxing activities. Try humming with your mouth closed. Put your palm on one side of your face and feel the slight vibration of your jawbone. Then lightly touch your nostrils with your thumb and index finger as if starting to pinch your nose and hum again, this time feeling the light but insistent vibration of your nostrils as the air streams out of your nose. You can also try the so-called humming bee breath meditation (*bhramri pranayam*): close your eyes, plug your ears with your index fingers, and hum out a few breaths to amplify these soothing vibrations.

Preloading on Smell and Flavor

While all smelling is inhalation, not all inhalation is smelling. What turns the in-breath into an act of smelling is the presence of the mind. Smelling is an act of information processing. Therefore mindless smelling isn't really smelling. Put differently, smelling is breathing in (inhaling) with attention.

Smelling is a distal sense: it allows us to touch (that is, to sense and thus to know) an object at a distance. So to smell food is to touch food from a distance. Therefore, smelling is the beginning of eating. Perhaps then it isn't surprising that conscious, mindful, attentive smelling can be a way to prime a sense of fullness and thereby preload the senses and prevent overeating.

Alan Hirsch, MD, an American physician who developed the Sensa appetite control method, found that consciously and mindfully smelling food before eating facilitates a sense of fullness and thus reduces the amount eaten. According to Hirsch (1998), the brain correlates the amount of aroma we inhale with the amount of the food we take in. Apparently the more you smell the food, the less of it you'll eat. Does that sound too good to be true? Put your nose to the test.

Try This: Take a Noseful, Not a Mouthful

The next several times you eat, try out a "noseful, not mouthful" approach, preloading on the smell before loading up on the food. It's also helpful to pause between bites for an additional noseful or two.

Try This: Warm Up Your Fullness

According to Alan Hirsch, hot meals give off more of an aroma than cold dishes (1988). With this in mind, try to warm up your sense of fullness with a steaming cup of bouillon. (Vegetarians, don't fret; you can experiment with plant-based bouillon cubes.) But rather than consuming the bouillon, simply allow it to fill you up with aroma. Take a few conscious whiffs of the steam and mmm them out through your nose. Fire up your satisfaction!

Try This: Eat with Your Nose

The smell of food accounts for a lion's share of the food's overall flavor. Smelling *is* eating. When you smell a given food, no matter how far away your nose might be from it, you are, in fact, coming in direct contact with the miniscule amounts of that food's particles that roam into your nasal passages. So if you smell chocolate, even if there's no chocolate in sight, let alone in your mouth, there's already chocolate in your nose and on your mind. Try taking a few conscious nosefuls before you eat. Try "eating with your nose" as a way of both relaxing and preloading.

Bringing It All Together: Take a Deep Whiff and Mmm It Out!

I've offered a lot of techniques to help you experiment with the relaxing and preloading aspects of breathing. Now here's a way to integrate them as your first course of the meal: Set out the food you plan to eat, then set your body. Spend a few minutes taking deep and conscious breaths. Each inhalation will double as diaphragmatic breathing and nasal preloading. As you exhale, hum-mmm out the air. That way each exhalation will serve to turbocharge relaxation (through NO release) and pleasure. What a way to pack a relaxation punch!

Worry not; while there is a lot going on here conceptually, behaviorally it's pretty straightforward. Let's walk through this little routine again: You are sitting at a table with food in front of you. You begin your meal with a course of relaxation, which involves taking a deep, conscious whiff of the food in front of you, allowing the air to fill your lungs as your diaphragm expands downward. Next, you exhale with a prolonged, satisfied mmm-ing hum through your nose. In, a lungful; out, an mmm-ful noseful.

Give it a try right now. Practice a satisfying breathing cycle of inhaling relaxation and exhaling stress. Inhale aromas and exhale satisfaction, through your nose if you can, or through pursed lips if need be. How long should you do this? Not long at all—just a couple of minutes. The nice thing about this is that you don't even have to set any time aside for this powerful relaxation and preloading combination. You just build it right into your eating ritual, assuring that you have a chance to experience a dose of profound relaxation exactly when it works the best: when your stomach is empty, right before you eat. Revel in the fact that you are accomplishing so much with so little: reducing stress in general; reducing or preventing any stress-based or emotional eating; preventing overeating by preloading on smell; and allowing yourself a moment of conscious satisfaction and pleasure in savoring the moment and the aroma of the food.

Breathing In as Fullness Awareness Training

Taking a deep, abdominal breath is an excellent way to prime your mind to notice the sensation of fullness. Satiety awareness or fullness awareness (or somatic monitoring, as I sometimes call it) is one of the essential skills of mindful eating. We can conceptualize fullness as being on a kind of continuum. Almost immediately after you eat a couple of mouthfuls of food, the sensation of hunger goes away (assuming you were hungry when you started eating). This is a moment of hunger relief. If you keep eating past this point, soon you'll begin to notice the pleasant distention of your stomach as it fills with food. This onset of pleasant fullness is generally a good time to stop eating.

Stopping when you're less than fully full or only pleasantly full is, in fact, one of the secrets of long and healthy life. In his book *Blue Zones: Lessons for Living Longer from the People Who've Lived the Longest* (2008), explorer and longevity expert Dan Buettner explains the *hara hachi bu* principle of the Okinawan elders, renowned for their longevity: stop eating when your stomach is 80 percent full. If you keep eating past the onset of pleasant fullness, you end up getting unpleasantly, if not painfully, stuffed. To keep that from happening, practice paying attention to the gradual distention of your stomach as it heralds the emerging onset of fullness. Taking a few deep, abdominal breaths and focusing on your stomach region at the outset of the meal will help prime your mind to focus on the soon-to-come distention of your stomach.

Try This: Simulate Fullness to Recognize Fullness

To practice satiety awareness, when you sit down to a meal take a few deep whiffs (to preload on smell). Exhale through your nose, mmm-ing and humming to increase both satisfaction and nitric oxide release. After a couple of breaths, consciously notice that the abdominal distention you feel as you inhale is the sensory signature of fullness. Stay attuned to it as you begin to eat. Note to yourself, "There it is; that's my fullness cue," as you feel your abdomen expand. By simulating the sensation of fullness before you eat in this way, you can learn to recognize the onset of fullness later during the meal.

Try pushing the envelope a bit: take a particularly deep abdominal breath, allowing your belly to expand out as far as it can. Notice the subtle tension and heaviness that come with this abdominal distention. This is, approximately, the danger zone between the far end of pleasant fullness and the beginning of feeling painfully stuffed. Using a moment of deep breathing to remind yourself of this overdistended sensation before the meal will help you learn to stop eating before you get too full.

Air, Then Water

So far we've been discussing breath-focused relaxation. However, the first course of relaxation isn't complete without the relaxing, preloading, and satiety-priming benefits of drinking water. I'll explain those benefits in a moment, but first try the following awareness-building experiences.

Try This: Experience the Water Block

It's best to do this on an empty stomach, or at least when you aren't too full. Pour yourself two large glasses of water. Take a few deep, abdominal breaths. Notice how relatively easy this is. Next, drink one entire glass of water, then try to take a deep, abdominal breath. Notice the subtle reduction in your breathing capacity. With water filling up your stomach, the diaphragm isn't as free to expand downward. As a result, your breaths feel shallower. Now drink the second glass of water, then try to take a deep, abdominal breath again. Notice the progression: deep, abdominal breathing has become increasingly difficult. Having a stomach full of water partially blocks the diaphragm from allowing you a deep, relaxing breath. You are, in essence, too full to fully relax.

This has a couple of implications: If you want to leverage maximum relaxation before you eat, start with air (deep breathing), not water. Air first; water second. Also, recognize that the act of drinking water, just like smelling mindfully, has a preloading function. It creates a sense of fullness even before you start eating, which is, of course, handy in terms of preventing overeating.

Try This: Study the Interplay of Breathing and Drinking

Pour a glass of water but don't drink it just yet. Simply notice your breathing, letting it be exactly as it is; there's no need to modify it. Next, take a sip of water and notice what happens to your breathing as you do so: it stops. Your lungs pause to allow you to take a breath. Drink the entire glass of water like this, one small sip at a time, noticing the effect on your overall pattern of breathing. You're likely to notice that your breathing slows down and that you begin to feel relaxed. The body is smart. It doesn't want you to choke. It pauses for you to take a sip and in so doing relaxes itself.

Preloading on Water

Research suggests that preloading by drinking two eight-ounce glasses of water before meals may help with weight-loss success (Davy et al. 2008). Another point of interest is that not drinking enough water reduces the activity of nitric oxide synthase, an enzyme that converts the amino acid L-arginine into nitric oxide, that miracle molecule of relaxation (Bryan and Zand 2010). Given the many potential benefits of drinking water just before a meal, you'll undoubtedly be eager to try the following preloading and satiety-priming experiences so you can experience them firsthand.

Try This: Feel the Power of Water

Hunger operates more like an alarm system than an indicator of how much we need to eat (Craighead 2006). Just because you feel extremely hungry doesn't mean you have to eat a lot. Next time you feel the pangs of hunger, have a sip of water and notice how the urgency of your hunger subsides. Nifty, huh? That's water power for you! If you're really famished, down a couple of glasses of water and see if the sensation of hunger is still there.

Try This: Put Out the Fire of Stress

Drinking water is a great coping technique. It's simple and can be an effective aid to relaxing. As noted above, in preparation for drinking the body involuntarily modifies the breath in a way that's relaxing. Plus, having a sip of cold water just feels relaxing. The sensation of water going down is like a caressing hand. When stressed, have a sip of water to notice how water strokes and soothes the throat and cools the stress-parched mouth. In addition, slowly drinking a glass of water is a process that can buy you a moment of contemplative nondoing. So have a glass of water to wash away feelings of being overwhelmed.

Try This: Water the World

We are entering the age of Aquarius, the water giver. Experiment with becoming a water giver yourself. Before your next meal, pour a tall glass of water and use it to water anything you think might need water, while also taking a sip from the very same glass as you walk around your home or yard. Water any plant and also take a sip from the same source. Pour some of the water from your glass into your pet's water bowl and then take another sip for yourself from the glass. Share a bit of the water from the glass with a tree or a blade of grass while intermittently taking sips for yourself. If you have no plants, pets, or yard, go outside with a bottle of water and find the nearest tree, bush, or plant and play with this routine there. Meditate on what's going on: we animals run on water, just like all other living matter on this planet. Ponder this common denominator as you share this precious resource. Recognize that to give water is to give life, to share water is to share a connection, and to see how we are alike is to transcend our differences. Be Aquarius.

Try This: Experience the Body Bottle

Recall that we are essentially living tubes. Yes, conscious, even spiritual, but still more or less tubes. There is no better way to experience this than to down a glass of cool water on an empty stomach. So wait until you feel empty, then pour a glass or two into yourself. Notice the water sliding down your throat. Feel it fill you up. Move your abdomen in and out to slosh it around. You see, your body is just like a bottle (which is why we call the bottle's opening a neck). Of course, unlike an actual bottle, you have an exit in addition to an entrance, which makes you a tube with valves. "And this means what?" you might wonder. Not much, just a reality check of reconnecting with your body. Input, output—appreciate the fundamental simplicity behind the complexity of these bodily details. You are an open system, your valves are a kind of swinging door through which the flow of life passes.

Shunryu Suzuki, a renowned Zen master, once wrote, "If you think, 'I breathe,' the 'I' is extra. There is no you to say 'I.' What we call 'I' is just a swinging door which moves when we inhale and when we exhale. It just moves; that is all. When your mind is pure and calm enough to follow this movement, there is nothing: no 'I,' no world, no mind nor body; just a swinging door" (2010, 11–12). The same is true when you drink: you are not what passes through you. You are not even the thought "I drink," let alone the thought "I am just like a bottle" or "I am a living tube." All of that is just information that streams through you. But what is this "you"? Who is this who is breathing, drinking, eating, and reading this? You'll have to wait until the second course—connecting with your mind (chapter 3)—to chew on this existential calorie. In the meantime, just fill up the body bottle and contemplate.

Empty Your Mind to Preempt Emotional Overeating

Relaxation as the first course of the meal has the added benefit of preventing emotional overeating and stress-based binge eating. When you're stressed, the mind is overwhelmed—that is, full of psychologically distressing thoughts. You can empty your mind with a helping of breath-focused relaxation, a serving of water, or both.

Try This: Fill Up on Your Body to Empty Your Mind

To relax, de-stress, and prime yourself for a mindful eating moment, first empty your mind. Make room for presence. Prime your hunger for an experience, and then fill up on the moment. Let your mind be as empty as a bowl before you fill it with soup. Mindful, relaxed eating is eating with an empty mind, so empty your mind before you fill your stomach. But how?

The best way to empty your mind is to fill up on your body. What does that mean? It means focusing on whatever currently is. What does that mean? It means using your senses—that is, sensing, not thinking. That's why I encourage you to start every meal with a first course of body-focused relaxation. And because breath is body, breath-focused relaxation is body-focused relaxation. Focus on the body of your breath to empty your mind. Understand that mindfulness is not fullness of mind, but emptiness of mind, a state of mind that's equal to a state of body. As you notice your breath, recognize that there is nothing but this moment. There is no past; there is no future. There is only this moment, and that's enough. Whatever was no longer is. Whatever might be isn't yet. But here you are, your living, breathing body. This body is the very ground of your existence from which your mind flowers. Notice your breath to center yourself. There is no better reality check than the sensation of air passing in and out of your nose.

Try This: Experience the Now of Eating

Eating is always in the present. We cannot eat in the past or in the future. We can only eat right now. When you sit down to eat, recognize the now of eating. Whatever has happened (good or bad) is already gone. The same is true of you: you have moved beyond that which was and have arrived into that which is. Placing awareness on your breath is permission from you to you to just be you. In this very moment, you are free to just be. Nothing, absolutely nothing, has to be different right now. Right now is a totally unique time—a time upon its own self, a now! Each now is a moment of breath, a time of metabolic and psycho-spiritual renewal: "To breathe in is to begin again" (Roche 2001, 14).

Relaxation Menu

Up to this point in the chapter, I've given you a lot of small morsels to digest. You've had a chance to experiment with a variety of awareness-building exercises that helped you directly experience key concepts. Now it's time to finalize the menu for relaxation and reconnecting with the body—the first course of the new meal. Try all of the practices that follow and begin to integrate them into your meals.

Practice: Abdominal Breathing

Cultivate the habit of beginning your meals with at least one conscious, mindful, diaphragmatic breath. Aim to begin your meals with a lungful: today, one lungful prior to every meal; tomorrow, two lungfuls prior to every meal; the day after tomorrow, three lungfuls prior to every meal. Each day, add one more lungful prior to every meal until you're up to seven lungfuls. Why seven? It adds up to only about one minute of your time. Perhaps you wonder if you should stop at seven or keep adding more lungfuls. Seven's enough. It's a number of harmony, after all.

Practice: Olfactory Preloading

Start getting into the habit of taking one conscious, mindful whiff of the food in front of you before you begin to eat. Complement your mouthfuls with a noseful, making sure to fill up on smell before you begin eating. Today have one noseful prior to every meal, tomorrow have two nosefuls prior to every meal, and work up to seven nosefuls. Why seven? A noseful is half of a breath (smelling is paying attention to what we inhale, so a whiff is a mindful in-breath). Simple, right? This takes only one more minute of your time, in addition to one minute of lungfuls.

Practice: Intentional Savoring

Begin to develop the habit of mmm-ing out at least one noseful of satisfaction. Just before you begin to eat, declare your satisfaction with an mmm-ing hum. Allow yourself a conscious foodgasm. Starting today, hum out one foodgasm worth of mmm-oaning prior to every meal. Add one more mmm-oment of savoring per day to build up to a total of seven mmms before each meal. Why seven? I think you already know. A hum is but half of a breath, the out-breath. So seven mmms adds up to only about one more minute of your time. So, yes, at the end of the week you'll have three whole minutes sunk into this routine: one minute of seven lungfuls, one minute of seven nosefuls, and one minute of seven mmm-n-mmms.

Practice: Taking a Super-Minute

What's that you say? You don't have three minutes to spare? Okay then, here's a time-saver: practice well-constructed lungfuls that are half noseful, half mmm-ful. A lungful is a mindful breath, the first half of which is a noseful on the in-breath, and the second half of which is a humming mmm-oan of delight on the out-breath. You can accomplish all three previous practices—abdominal breathing, olfactory preloading, and intentional savoring—in one set of seven breaths. However, doing so will require your full attention. I call this a super-minute.

Instead of doing seven lungfuls, then seven nosefuls, and then seven mmm-fuls over a span of three minutes, you can pack all of this into one minute. How? By mindfully smelling as you take a deep abdominal breath and by humming out with delight as you exhale.

Practice: Liquid Preloading

Get into a habit of preloading on water. Right after you have a lungful, a noseful, and an mmm-ful foodgasm, have a full glass of water. Take your time drinking. How much time? How much time do you have for yourself, busy bee? That much.

Practice: Fullness Awareness

Practice distending your abdomen as you take deep, abdominal breaths, and feel the fullness in your stomach as you preload on water. Recognize these feelings of distention and fullness as cues to watch for later, when you eat. As you take deep, diaphragmatic lungfuls or drink water prior to eating, make a conscious note to yourself: "There it is, the distention, just like fullness. I'll need to be on the lookout for this as I eat."

Practice: Taking Your Stress Pulse

Spend the next couple of weeks taking your stress pulse before you eat. As you sit down to a meal, ask yourself, "Am I at risk for emotional eating?" If you feel particularly stressed and at risk for emotional over-eating or binge eating, double up on your relaxation appetizer. Take a few extra lungfuls, give yourself an extra helping of conscious nosefuls, and indulge in two or more additional and emphatic mmm-ing food-gasms to deepen the relaxation with the help of extra nitric oxide release. Also remind yourself that in this moment, right now, there is nothing but breath, nothing but this sip of water, nothing but this aroma of food. Everything else can wait. Empty your mind to preempt emotional overeating.

Practice: An On-the-Go Relaxation Shortcut

For the super-busy among us and for times when you have to eat on the go, here's a mini relaxation (adapted from Benson and Proctor 2010, 116): Take a deep, abdominal breath and hold it for several seconds. Herbert Benson recommends holding the breath for seven to ten seconds before you exhale, but I wouldn't worry too much about time-keeping at this point. Simply allow yourself to settle into a brief pause after you inhale. Then exhale through your nose or pursed lips and, as you do so, mentally repeat a focus word or phrase to yourself. Consider such cue words as "relax," "calm," "peace," "om," or (my favorite) "just this." Choose something brief, soothing, and grounding. You can turbocharge Benson's mini relaxation practice by humming out the air with your eyes closed. Taking just a single breath in this way is an excellent shortcut to relaxation.

If You Have Time to Eat, You Have Time to Relax

Ditch the excuse that you don't have time for relaxation or stress-management. If you have time to eat—and you obviously do—you have time to relax. In fact, if you take just three to five minutes to relax before you eat three times a day, you'll be spending ten to fifteen minutes a day in breath-focused contemplation. That's a solid self-care routine. You don't have to hustle for time to create a separate, stand-alone stress-management routine. You already have a stress-management, self-care routine. It's called eating. Simply add a course of relaxation to it.

If you don't have five minutes (for seven lungfuls, seven nosefuls, seven mmm-ful moans of pleasure, and a moment or two of satiety awareness), then do a super-minute, combining a noseful and an mmm-ful into each mindful lungful. I'm sure that you can always find at least that much time for yourself before you eat. So retire your favorite excuse: not having enough time. You don't need any extra time here. You already make time to eat several times a day. You simply need to repurpose the time you already take for mindless overeating, on the back end of the meal, for a first course of mindful relaxation. Who knows, you might even save yourself some time—or gain some time— by hopefully sticking around for a few years longer.

Conclusion: A Vision of Self-Nourishing Self-Care

Recall that the new meal is a total body-mind self-care event—one to be repeated whenever you're ready to eat. This comprehensive self-care activity of self-nourishment begins with a course of turbocharged relaxation that involves conscious and mindful intake of air and water. Imagine for a moment a flow of five streams: a stream of breath, a stream of water, a stream of relaxation, a stream of health, and a stream of pleasure. Imagine these streams joining together into one inseparable stream of well-being flowing through your core.

This is what the first course of relaxation attempts to create. It brings together the currents of stress management and the currents of physical attunement into one course—one flow of self-nourishing self-care. And it accomplishes all of this without you having to set aside any separate time for self-care. Rather, relaxation is built right into the routine of eating that is already in place. This entire first course of reconnecting with your body need not take more than several minutes at the outset of your meal.

Imagine a time in the not-too-distant future when you've cultivated this routine, taking a few moments for yourself two or three times a day without taking any extra time out of your busy life. This nominal addition of several minutes will have an amazing ripple effect. This perfectly timed breath-focused relaxation (occurring when your stomach is empty and therefore allowing for an unobstructed diaphragmatic breath) is turbocharged with nitric-oxide-activating hums of pleasure in a physiologically smart, elegantly time-efficient, emotionally wise, and reasonably self-indulging first course of relaxation that will help you stay on the course of mindfulness.

An Amuse-Bouche of Pattern Interruption

So here you are, at the end of another chapter. I hope you're off to a good start. Before you rush into another chapter, cleanse the palate of your mind with a few meditative mindfuls. The "prescription" couldn't be any simpler: open your mind before you open your mouth. How? Start your next several meals with the pattern-interruption appetizers below. Make the eating zombie within get up on the wrong side of the bed. Then enjoy the enlightening confusion of the eating moment that follows.

Eating Is Taking

Eating is metabolically self-serving. We literally devour the environment. We take what we need—matter, energy, life—and we expel what we don't need. As such, eating is a one-way transaction, a "one-way traffic of food" (La Barre 1954, 10). So who should you thank? Earth? Self? Both? No one? I'll leave it up to you to figure out.

Eating Is Destructive

In eating, we take in order and generate waste. Indeed, life creates life and then life itself destroys it. The Universe grows a beautiful orange. Then we peel it, eat it, and destroy it. Eating is a chemical-mechanical process of demolition. Nothing's wrong with that. It's just something to think about as you work your jaws.

Eating Is Intimacy

Eating is touch. We first smell (a micro form of touch) and taste (a macro form of touch) the environment. After this sensory kiss, we ingest the environment, and then it touches us inside as we allow it in deep inside us, like a lover's tongue. Eating is intimacy between ego and eco. Eating is sex; eating is union; eating is pleasure. Partake.

Eating Is a Flow

Consider, for a moment, a pipe with water running through it. Is the outflow different from the inflow? Yes and no. Our dualistic minds can certainly separate this unified process of water flowing through a tube into two aspects: inflow and outflow. But that's just the mind at work. It likes to cut up the oneness of what is into unnecessary dichotomies. In reality, the inflow and the outflow are one and the same flow. Now, consider eating and shitting. These aren't truly two; they are one. Sure, we can look at eating and shitting as two separate processes. Or we can sober up to the fact that the eating and shitting are just the inflow and outflow of the food stream that runs through the tubes that we are. Just because it takes time for this food stream to pass from one end to the other doesn't mean that it isn't one and the same stream. So before you open up the intake of your digestive tract, consider the "inconvenient" truth that this flow of food feels good on both ends. It feels good to fill up on what we need, and it feels good to get rid of what we don't need. To take this line of thought one step further, consider the hydra—small freshwater organisms with an earlier evolutionary gastrointestinal design. In these simple creatures, the mouth doubles as an anus. Not a particularly savory thought, but certainly full of pattern-interruption calories!

The Food-River That Runs Through Us

Neurophysiologist and behavioral scientist Ralph Gerard once wrote, "The structure and function of an organism have often been compared to a river bed and a river, and many shrewd analogies exist between the stream of life and that of water. One cannot say simply that the banks control the flow or the stream its channel, for each acts upon the other and react in turn upon itself... [A] river which is dry most of the year ages more slowly than one with a continuous flow" (1961, 322–323). The same is true of the flow of food through the riverbed of your digestive tract. Just as the water streaming through a riverbed erodes the river's banks, the very food that sustains us also eventually kills us.

Eating is an energy-production process, and energy production is one of the causes of free radicals. According to Hari Sharma, MD, in his book *Freedom from Disease*, "The most likely reason that metabolizing less food [calorie restriction] increases life span is the correlation between metabolism and free radical production" (1993, 30). In Sharma's words, "Burning calories is ultimately a self-limiting process" (1993, 52). Eating is a source of metabolic wear and tear, and the faster the food river runs, the less time it endures.

Share your mindful eating experiences online using the Mindful Eating Tracker at http://www.eatingthemoment.com/mindfulness-tracker.

chapter 3

Second Course: Reconnecting with Your Mind

Do not let ice form on the free flowing waters of innate awareness by sticking to old holding patterns or by resting quietly in temporarily pleasant states of mind such as nonthought, bliss, or clarity; break these up by looking into who is peaceful, who is thought-free, who is blissful. And then suddenly drop everything and let go, release, breathe deeply, and start again—fresh, vividly present, wakeful.

— Lama Surya Das, *Natural Radiance*

The old-school meal begins with the opening of the mouth. The new meal begins with a course of relaxation and proceeds with the opening of the mind. The first course of the new meal is a course of relaxation, and the second is a serving of self. Put differently, the first course of relaxation helps you rediscover your body, and the second course helps you rediscover the discoverer: yourself. The second course is soul food, an appetizer of "am-ness," a serving of existential calories. In brief, the second course of the new meal focuses not on the food but on the eater. This is key. Before you can focus on the process of eating itself (the third course, discussed in chapter 4), you—the eater—have to learn to show up for the eating moment.

A Word about Confusion

Confusion, as I see it, is a prerequisite to clarity. Confusion is when you don't know what is what. When you don't know what is what, your mind is open to what actually is, as opposed to what you thought was the case. As such, confusion is a release of categories. It's liberation from the certainties that box us into clichéd thought patterns. It's the beginning of a jailbreak from the prison of words. So tolerate it. Better yet, embrace it. That's the only path to clarity, which is not to be confused with certainty. We have to create *a clearing of mind* so you can learn to see *you*—a viewpoint that will help keep you from getting lost in the dizzying mindlessness of yet another old-school meal event.

As I explain what the second course of this new meal is all about, I ask you for the benefit of the doubt. I am not being unnecessarily confusing—not at all. I am being *necessarily* confusing. This is the best path I know for helping you past the confusion of words. I'm not just being a rascal; I'm using an approach that works. You might say it's a type of conversational hypnosis: You and I walk down a hallway of words. I point to a word door to your side and encourage you to go inside, into the mind room beyond words. And you say, "But this word door has no meaning-handle!" I say, "Exactly!" Then, maybe a lightbulb of insight goes off in your mind. If it doesn't, no big deal. We can look for another door.

Meditation Course

After you've enjoyed a first course of relaxation, having noticed your body and being ready to eat, is good time to ask yourself, "Who's going to eat, me or an eating zombie?" Hopefully you—the conscious you, not you on autopilot. Hopefully the mindful, self-aware, fully present you, not the mindless, hand-to-mouth habitual you. Here's the speed bump that can help you slow down and become present: asking yourself what this conscious you is, that is posing the question to your own self. The question to ask yourself before you open your mouth is "Who am I? What is this sense of presence that I call 'myself'?

The second course is meditation, which enlightens. Whereas the first course of the new meal, relaxation, relaxes the body and the mind, meditation enlightens, revealing that body and mind are one, that the word "body" and the word "mind" refer to one and the same being—a being that is beyond words. Relaxation eases the body-mind duality. Meditation collapses the body-mind duality into one unhyphenated notion of bodymind and then, as if that weren't enough, takes you beyond the verbal, straight down into the rabbit hole of am-ness.

Why bother with this kind of premeal self-discovery? It's essential to transforming a mindless meal into a total bodymind self-care routine:

1. First course: relaxation

2. Second course: meditation

3. Third course: eating mindfully

The sequence matters. It's hard to show up for the act of eating, to be the eater, when you're tense, caught up in stress, or preoccupied with something other than eating—in other words, when something is eating at you. The first course of relaxation allows you to release the past. The second course allows you to get rooted in the present. Eating itself is what follows.

But how do you do this meditation thing? That is always the question. And notice how questions generate questions. First we asked, "Who's going to eat, me or an eating zombie?" That led to the question

"Who am I? What is this sense of presence that I call 'myself'?" Consider this: questions are quests, and all quests involve moving forward. A question is a current of inquiry, a vector of attention. As you move forward, the horizon always retreats and the road always extends. The same is true of word quests: as you move forward in your inquiry, the inquiry horizon of the unknown keeps retreating and the word path keeps extending. So what are we to do? How are we to get there, to where we want to be? Notice that these are more questions that beg answers.

The answer is a nonanswer. The answer is to let go of the question. The answer is to realize that you already are where you want to be, that you have already gotten there, that you have already arrived, that you have always been arriving. The answer is to stop the quest, if only for this moment, to stop searching for self amidst word-based self-descriptions. This is the point of this second course of meditation: to rediscover the preverbal or nonverbal life current that courses through you and is you. The idea is to finally serve yourself a sense of self that we are all so famished for. The point of the second course is to let go of any point, if only for a moment—to get off the treadmill of time and awaken to the ordinary timelessness of your essence. In the second course, you eat the moment, filling up on the am-ness calories and becoming the moment.

Yes, this is all still just words. You're probably looking for something tangible. Yet words are all I can give you, whether we meet in a book or in session. However, you don't have to stop at my words. You can take them and use them to go beyond the words to the inexpressible immediacy of experience. In fact, you can do that right now by noticing the very you that is reading these words.

There is nothing academic or informational about this meditation course. There's nothing to learn here, no new ideas, and no new facts, just the same-old sameness of presence. The meditation course of the new meal isn't a course of learning. It's a realization that there's nothing to learn right now. It's a recognition of the life that courses through you—and of yourself as that very current that you now recognize. This takes tolerance for self-referencing, for circularity and paradox. You are both the one that is noticing yourself (the subject) and the one you are noticing (the object). And you are neither.

On a practical level, all that's necessary here is to figure how to access it. (By "it," I mean "you." Figuring out what I mean by "you" is up to…you.) All that's needed is for you to realize that a meal is not a meal without an eater, and that you are not a "you" without the essential you—the life current that transcends words. The old meal was, at best, filling. The new meal is self-fulfilling. It allows you to reconnect with your essential self, to go off autopilot and reenter this body that's been running mindlessly on the fumes of old habits.

A Serving of Rig-Veda

Consider this verse from the Rig-Veda, an ancient Indian text of sacred hymns (de Nicolas 1976, 66):

Two birds with fair wings, inseparable companions,
have found a refuge in the same sheltering tree.
One incessantly eats from the fig tree;
The other, not eating, just looks on.

What is this enigmatic passage about? Who is this other bird that is not eating and is just looking on? The message is that eating is inevitable but mindfulness isn't. When we use eating as an opportunity to awaken ourselves from a zombie state, we stand to glimpse that elusive, essential sense of self—that silent bird of consciousness—that witnesses our day-to-day feeding frenzy.

So what am I proposing? A simple thing, really. At your next meal, after a first course of relaxation but before you eat, ask yourself, "Who is this who is about to start eating? Who is this who, in this very moment, is governing the amazing machinery of flesh that is gearing up for eating? Who is this who is silently supervising this joint-and-tendon marionette, this puppet of the body, as it lifts fork, knife, and spoon, then chews, then swallows? Who is this who is now asking, 'Who is this?'" As you struggle to answer this recursive question that folds back onto itself, know that you are looking straight into your original face. You are acknowledging that fundamental, inexpressible, yet very real sense of self-presence. And this "you," this bird of mindfulness that is looking on, is always full, complete, and lacking nothing whatsoever in its primordial satisfaction. Then, having felt self-fulfilled, let go of the question.

One Taste

Chogyal Norbu, a master of the Tibetan Buddhist Dzogchen tradition, said, "We don't understand in an intellectual way how sugar tastes. If we have never had the experience of sugar, we don't know what 'sweet' is. We can read many books introducing us to the meaning of 'sweet,' and we can learn and construct many ideas, but we can never have a concrete experience of 'sweet' in this way." But, he adds, "If we get a small piece of chocolate and place it on our tongue, we can have a concrete experience" (2006, 113).

Norbu isn't really talking about the taste of chocolate; he's talking about the taste of self. So here you are: relaxed, with food in front of you, and about to eat it mindfully, but stuck in this confusing intermediate step of trying to have a taste of self. What to do? Have an actual taste. Choose something from the table and taste it, and as you taste it, ask yourself, "Who is this who is having this taste?" That's right, have a taste of you tasting the not-you (the food before you). Typically, mindful eating is all about noticing the food and paying attention to eating. That's fine, but that's the third course of the new meal. Right now, have a taste of self and notice you the eater, you the taster, and you the noticer. You are that which is tasting the not-you (the food that is about to become you).

Removing the Quotation Marks

Imagine I have an apple in my hand and ask you, "What is this?" You say, "It's an apple, of course!" I give you an "Are you sure?" look and then take a bite and proceed to mindfully consume it, taking my time. Then I muse out loud, "What just happened? There was an apple, and there was me. We were separate. We arrived at this moment by different paths. We were independent. But then I took a bite of this apple and now this apple is in me, being digested and metabolized, becoming me, and now being me. When a piece of this apple is being digested inside of me, is it still an apple or is it already 'me'? What's clear is that, right now, this apple applies to me as much as it applies to its own self. And once I eat it in its entirety, this 'it,' this apple, is indistinguishable from whatever it is that I call 'me.'"

Recall how this whole verbal mess started. A moment ago I asked you to imagine me holding an apple, and then I described a vision of the apple becoming me—or, if you look at it from the other side, a vision of me becoming the apple. As you were reading through this collapse of duality, in which two things were becoming one, you might have envisioned me going on and on about this silliness using annoying air quotes around all the seemingly self-evident words: "apple," "it," "I," "me," "we." And then you might have wondered, "How does all of this apply to me?" That's a good question. This question is a thought you had while reading and visualizing my thoughts. So here's my question to you: Who is thinking this very thought that you're thinking? And if you happen to be thinking, "I am," then let me follow up with this question: And who is thinking the thought "I am"?

Notice how the same process as in the apple-and-me story above is happening between me and you. To you, I am this book right now. As you are reading it, this "it" is becoming you. I became an apple. You are becoming this thought. My point is this: any time you come in contact with reality (which is always), the apparent duality of you and not-you collapses. The meaning of words begins to dissolve and the air quotes become irrelevant. When you are eating, you are the one who is eating, the food that you're consuming, and the very behavior of eating that you're engaged in. You are simultaneously the subject that acts, the object you act upon, and the act itself. You are the entire trinity of the moment.

Once again, you might be scratching your head, wondering, "But how does this apply to eating?" There is a concept of eating here, but no actual, stand-alone eating. Understand that there is no eating separate from you the eater. Nor is there any eater separate from the food you are eating, because there can be no eating without food and there can be no eater without eating. Reread this until you understand. Consider the Rig-Veda mantra *Tat tvam asi*, a morsel of Sanskrit that means "You are that." When you eat an apple, you are the one eating it, you are the act of eating, and you are that which you eat—you are the apple. So as you set out to taste yourself, see how what you are tasting applies to you, because it literally does. You are that which you are experiencing, be it the aroma of the food in front of you or the hopefully enlightening confusion of this sentence.

Try This: Have an Atman Sandwich

Have a taste of some food in front of you and let the tongue of mindfulness speak the language of self-recognition. In *Blooming of a Lotus*, Vietnamese Buddhist monk Thich Nhat Hanh wrote, "Aware of my tongue, I breathe in. Aware of the taste…, I breathe out" (1993, 41). Recognize that you, this taste, and the act of tasting—all of the elements of this tasting moment—are passing. Recognize yourself in this flow of impermanence and stir up the pot of contemplation with yet another "Who am I? What is passing?" Then drop the question to find the answer.

I think of this tug-of-war of pondering the imponderable as a sandwich of breath and spirit, or an "atman sandwich." The Latin root of the word "spirit" means "breath," and the Sanskrit word *atman* also means "breath." These words also have well-established psychospiritual connotations. The concept of spirit generally means "essence" or "true, essential self." The same is true of the word "atman," which in Hinduism also has the meaning "self." What we have here is a kind of psycholinguistic sandwich in which breath equates to self. Self is breath, and breath is self. I hope this clarifies even if it confuses.

So, as you keep asking yourself, "Who am I?" you are serving yourself a sandwich of meditation, that is, a sandwich of breath, which is a sandwich of self. The very question "Who am I?" streams from self-powering breath or, to reverse the emphasis, from breath-powered self. Once again, ask, "Who am I?" The very breath of the question—right now—is literally the answer: you are the breath. You are the very question you are asking, the very thought you are having, the very smell you are smelling, the very taste you are tasting. "Who am I?" is more of an answer than a question. It is a question that answers itself. That's the atman sandwich of it. Enjoy a bite.

Try This: Have a Serving of Self

Mindful self-awareness is just being. It isn't something you do; it's non-doing. Being—if already in progress—needs no doing. It (being, that is) already is. Whatever is, is already accomplished since it already exists. You already are. There is nothing else to accomplish for you to be you. So a moment of nondoing (meaning a conscious moment of being) is as good a definition of self as anything else is—as is a moment of non-eating. So having relaxed your body with a course of relaxation, look at the food you are about to eat and do nothing. Just be for a moment. Or ask yourself, "Who am I?" and leave the question unanswered. Ask a question and do nothing, since to do nothing is to remain in a state of being, which *is* the answer to the question "Who am I?" To ask, "Who am I?" and not answer *is* to answer—nonverbally. So, having relaxed your body with the first course, allow yourself to simply rest in the moment, doing nothing and leaving everything exactly as it is. Nothing is required of you, not even meditating. This is a nonmeditation meditation: being, in and of itself, is a silent answer to the question "Who am I?" It is a serving of self.

Try This: Fill Up on Am-Ness Calories

You've heard the phrase "food for thought." What about "thought for food"? So glad you asked. Let me tell you about that. Here I am, sharing my thoughts through these words. Here you are, reading. Let's both stop for a moment. Actually do it: stop reading.

Neither of us was doing anything in that moment, but both of us still were. Regardless of *what* we do, irrespective of *how* we are, there is always a sense of something permanent in this flow of impermanence, a sense of unqualified, inexpressible continuity of self. That's am-ness. It's self-sustaining. Being takes care of itself. It continues and renews itself, even when it is doing nothing. Being is its own food. I call this realization "an am-ness calorie." Having relaxed your body and now sitting with food in front of you and nothing to do, enjoy a course of unqualified existence. Let self-presence fill you. Have an "am-ful" and see that it's enough.

Practice Time

Up to this point in the chapter, I've given you a lot of words to digest. I've served up a confusion of words as an invitation to build awareness. Now, at last, I'll give you something a bit more tangible: the words below, which are an invitation to practice.

Practice: Popping the Question

In the weeks to come, after you set your food on the table and relax your bodymind with breathing, conscious smelling, and sipping water, pop the question: ask, "Who am I?" This act of asking isn't meditation. The nondoing that follows the question is the meditation. What is this meditation? It's a nonmeditation. Pop the question and leave it unanswered. Let the silence of your presence speak for itself.

Practice: Taking Time

Mindful eating isn't a *Minute to Win It* type of contest. But do take at least a minute to be mindfully you. In the weeks to come, after your first course of relaxation, as you sit with your food in front of you, take a minute to literally do nothing before you dig in. There's no rush; there isn't a million bucks to win. You don't even have to ask yourself any confusing questions. Just be rich in time. Give yourself a minute of simply being.

Practice: Taking a Taste

In the weeks to come, after your first course of relaxation and before you eat, have a taste of the food in front of you and allow this to become a taste of self. As you have a spoonful of soup, collapse the duality: Recognize that this soup is becoming you and you are becoming this soup. Recognize that in this moment of eating yoga, you are touching reality, reality is touching you, and the two of you are becoming one and the same reality. Put your mind, your mouth, and a taste of your meal on a collision course of oneness. Have yourself a serving of oneness, which is selfness, which is am-ness.

Conclusion: Full Yet?

Time for a recap. The new meal begins with a first course of relaxation. It proceeds with a second course of meditation (that is, with a course of just being). And it concludes with mindful eating (discussed in chapter 4). Together, these three courses comprise a total bodymind self-care event that you can engage in two to three times a day. More specifically, here's what's on the menu:

1. First course: relaxation and preloading. A few lungfuls and nosefuls of relaxation, and a few mmm-fuls of pleasure— basically air, water, relaxation, and pleasure. The focus is on breathing.

2. Second course: meditation. An am-ful or two, in other words, a moment of nondoing, a moment of nonverbal self-awareness provoked by asking, "Who is this? Who am I?" and leaving those questions unanswered. The focus is on simply being (that is, on simply being your conscious self, the eater).

3. Third course: food and presence. The food in front of you, enjoyed with mindfulness of flavor and of the process of eating. The focus is on food and eating.

A menu is a list of options. The new meal puts reconnecting with your body, reconnecting with your mind, and reconnecting with your world through food back on the menu. Mindful eating puts *you* back into the meal. And all of this at no time cost to speak of.

An Amuse-Bouche of Pattern Interruption

By now you know the drill: it's time to slow down and cleanse your mind's palate with a course of pattern interruption. How? Read and eat—not in parallel, not at the same time, but in sequence. Whenever you're ready to eat, first read one of the vignettes below as a meditative appetizer, and then eat. And fear not the philosophical indigestion that follows.

The Autonomy of Eating

As philosopher Gregory Sams astutely notes, "We cannot stop our heartbeat or our breathing but we can choose to stop eating and die, as many protest-fasters have demonstrated" (2009, 208). This is a fascinating point. If you were to try to hold your breath to kill yourself, you would faint and your body would take over the steering wheel of your existence, overriding your intention in a kind of body-over-mind coup d'état. But if you decide to stop eating, your body is out of luck. Sure, it will torment you with pangs of hunger, but without the assistance of your volition, it cannot move your hand to put food in its mouth. The behavior of eating is not only within your control, it is also the reins with which you steer this chariot of body. How marvelous!

If you choose not to fuel this vehicle of life, it dies. Ponder this the next time you sit down to a meal. Allow yourself to fully appreciate the significance of the moment when you begin to eat. The choice to eat is not the beginning of loss of control; rather, it's the very proclamation of self-control. You are in charge of this hapless mass of matter. You animate it with your decision to eat and therefore to live. Allow yourself to experience the moment before eating as a proclamation of autonomy—a moment of psychosomatic sovereignty and an assertion of self.

Eating the Family

Evolutionary biologist and Pulitzer Prize winner Edward O. Wilson once wrote, "Other species are our kin" (1993, 39). Indeed, all of us—from an ant to a sequoia and from a carnivorous plant to a vegetarian human—have evolved from a population of single-celled organisms that lived almost two billion years ago. How do we know this? "All this distant kinship is stamped by a common genetic code and elementary features of cell structure" (Wilson 1993, 39). What this means is that each and every time we sit down to a meal, we are eating our kin—eating our own Earth family. This is neither good nor bad; it simply is. Nature is beyond morality. Ponder this at your next meal to see if you can relate.

The Matter of Eating

Giordano Bruno, an astronomer, mathematician, and Dominican friar who lived in the sixteenth century, was one of the most daring minds in the history of humanity—and was burned alive by the Inquisition for his bold ideas. Among his truisms is one that speaks to the alchemy of eating: "Don't you see,...that which was seed will get green herb, and herb will turn into ear and ear into bread. Bread will turn into nutrient liquid, which produces blood, from blood semen, embryo, men, corpse, Earth, rock, and mineral and thus matter will change its form ever and ever and is capable of taking any natural form" (as quoted in Margulis and Sagan 1995, 91). The matter of eating is that we are eating matter. There is, of course, ambiguity in what I just said. Did I mean that we are eating *matter*, in the sense that we are having matter for breakfast, lunch, and supper? Or did I mean that we are *eating* matter, in the sense that we ourselves are matter (the stuff of life) that eats. Indeed, we are both, and Bruno's quote speaks to the fact that we are matter-eating matter.

Leftovers of Essence

Taoist sage Zhuangzi, thought to have lived in about the fourth century BCE, has been cited as saying, "When things come to us from the outside, it is only for a while. When they come we cannot hinder them; when they leave we cannot detain them" (Hochsmann and Guorong 2007, 66). That's certainly the case with food. You eat and you shit. Life is metabolic input and output. Have a grape or a square of chocolate and see how there is no holding on to it. It comes and it goes. The question is, what remains?

A Wave of Eating

Just like there is no ocean wave without water, there is no you without food. Imagine that you are, in fact, a wave—an ocean wave named Bob. To continue to be, you would need a continuous supply of water—constantly new water as you advance across the ocean. An ocean wave that runs out of water dies. The fascinating thing is this: here you are, an ocean wave named Bob, made entirely of water, but of ever-new water. As you realize this, you ponder, "If I started way back out there, made of that water, and now I am rolling toward the shore made of entirely different water, then who have I been throughout? If all I am is water, but never the same water, who the hell am I?" And then you remember: "Oh, right; I'm a wave named Bob."

The same is true of us humans—and of all beings. According to science writer and theorist Dorion Sagan, "Life is a wave" (1990, 25):

> With each breath you take, each bead of sweat that evaporates from your skin, or each scone that you consume you replace chemical constituents in your body. In no two consecutive moments are you or any other life form composed of exactly the same particles... Tracking the flow of the matter of life

guarantees that now in your body are atoms that once grew in the tree of Buddha, soiled the clothes of Jesus, and reflected as the eye of Picasso. As with the continuous recycling of water in the ocean to make waves, the pool of chemical elements from which we are made is finite. Matter, especially living matter, cycles.

So as you sit down for your next meal, ask yourself, "Who am I? Who is this?" And recognize that you are a wave of eating.

Share your mindful eating experiences online using the Mindful Eating Tracker at http://www.eatingthemoment.com/mindfulness-tracker.

chapter 4

Third Course: Reconnecting with Your World

Every rite has its irrational, mystical center, its acme of concentration, its moment out of time… Its purpose is ecstatic union, however fleeting, with transcendent reality, with the ultimate, with what is beyond mutability.

— Thomas Cahill, *The Gifts of the Jews*

The old-school meal begins with food, proceeds with mindless eating, and ends with feeling stuffed and existentially empty. The new meal begins with a first course of relaxation, proceeds with a second course of self-awareness, and then progresses into mindful, conscious, intimate appreciation of the world at large through food. As such, the third course of the new meal is about both mindful eating and mindful interbeing with all that immediately is. Having reconnected with your body and then with your essential self, the challenge is to stay in touch with the world as you consume it. Remember, when you're eating, you're eating Earth and becoming Earth. So the goal is to stay humble and not let your mind wing you away to the heavens of abstraction.

The goal is simply to just eat. However, while it's easy to say "just eat," it can be hard to do. The point of this chapter is to make it easier.

Mindfulness Is Awareness of Choice

Habits preempt choice. Once a given behavior goes on autopilot, we just keep on flying on the course set by habit. Making choices is work, and the mind often doesn't want to hassle with it. So it leaves the dirty work of making choices to the memory of the body. Mindless eating is basically muscle memory, whereas mindful eating is a series of mini choices.

The body itself makes no choices, it just repeats what it has done previously as trained by the mind. In terms of eating, we have pretty much trained ourselves to ignore eating. Watching TV or checking email is the steak we have for dinner; the food itself is just garnish. That's the wheel of automaticity, the wheel of mindlessness. Eating is one of the most overlearned voluntary behaviors in the human repertoire of skills. So let's breathe some mindful choice into this mindless choicelessness. In the meantime chew on this: mindlessness is choicelessness, whereas mindfulness is an awareness of choices, that is, choicefulness.

Try This: Draw the Circle of Choice

Get three sheets of paper and a pen. Draw a circle on each piece of paper, for a total of three circles.

Please don't read any further until you have drawn your three circles.

Once you've drawn your circles, look at them. Chances are you have drawn all three circles in more or less the same way. I bet that the placement of the circle on each page is similar, and that all three circles are somewhat similar in diameter. Most likely, you even drew all three by starting at the same point (probably somewhere in the upper right) and drawing them in the same direction. Did you *consciously* intend for these circles to be similar in terms of their placement on the page, their size, and even the starting point and direction in which you drew them? Probably not.

In a sense, *you* didn't draw these circles—habit did. These circles, as evidenced by their unintentional similarities, were drawn too mind-lessly, too reflexively, too mechanically, too robotically—ultimately, too unconsciously—for you to take full credit for this action. This was a *reaction*, meaning a reenactment of some circle-drawing habit. True action involves conscious deliberation. Realize that habits are just like these mindlessly drawn circles. They are mindless behavioral feedback loops that endlessly flow into and out of themselves.

If habits are the wheels that keep life spinning in circles, let's toss a monkey wrench into this circle cycle. I invite you to draw another circle. But this time, draw it mindfully, with the awareness of the options available to you. *Intend* the choices that you didn't make the first time. Choose where on the page to place the circle, choose the starting point, choose the direction in which you will draw the circle, choose the diameter of the circle, and even choose whether to bring the ends of the line together to make a full circle or not. Go ahead and do it and notice the difference.

=====

Enso Your Way into Eating

Enso is Japanese for "circle," a common subject of Zen calligraphy. An empty *enso* circle symbolizes enlightenment and the void (emptiness). Why void? Why enlightenment? An *enso* drawing, as I see it, docu-ments the fleeting insubstantiality of the moment and the enlightened awareness of its impermanence. As such, an *enso* drawing is a pattern interrupter. It is a moment of presence, or mindfulness, and a commit-ment to the moment, however fleeting it might be.

Most of us in the West eat off of circular plates. Next time you see the circular shape of a plate, think, "*enso!*" Think, "a symbol of void and emptiness not unlike my hunger." Think, "an opportunity for awareness!" Recognize the circular dish in front of you as an invaluable cue and ask yourself, "Will my next eating moment be just another mindless spin around this carousel of eating? Will it be another vicious cycle of mindless overeating? Will I spend the next ten minutes flipping through the menu circle of TV channels with untasted food in my mouth? Or will I break the pattern, select a new course, notice the moment, notice the world, touch reality, and see myself interact with it?" Before you find yourself mindlessly cleaning your plate, clean the cobwebs of routine patterns from your mind.

Try This: Put a Finger on It

You don't have to stop with *enso*-inspired thoughts. You can literally *enso* your way into eating. Whereas classic Zen *enso* calligraphy is brushwork, you can use your fingers. Put an empty plate in front of you and trace the rim of the plate with your finger. That's an *enso* finger painting—but a fairly mindless one. Now allow the empty plate in front of you to symbolize the void of your hunger, then make a conscious choice about whether you will trace it clockwise or counterclockwise. Then consciously choose a starting point and mindfully trace an *enso* of presence around the rim of the empty plate. Practice this *enso* routine as a rite of eating passage, a green light of presence and awareness, a way of giving yourself permission to proceed. Consider this *enso* moment as a kind of preflight inspection: "Here I am. I have showed up for this moment, fully myself, self-aware, and aware of my choices—an eater, not an eating zombie."

Pattern-Interruption Strategies

Choice-awareness training is intended both as a general tonic for promoting mindfulness and as a specific tool for leveraging more presence while you eat. The idea behind choice awareness and pattern interruption is to take you off of autopilot and keep you off. Mindlessness is blindness. Mindfulness is vision. Here are some approaches to help you loosen up your eating patterns and to help you see—with your mind's eye—what you are eating.

Try This: Eat with Your Nondominant Hand

Switch the hand you use to eat with. If you typically eat with a fork or spoon in your right hand, hold it in your left hand, and vice versa. Note the confusion of the mind and the increase in your level of mindfulness. Likewise, if using more than one utensil at a time, as with a knife and fork, switch hands to break up habitual eating patterns and to infuse more presence into the process of eating. .

Try This: Eat with Atypical Utensils

Utensils are part of the hypnotic ritual of eating. They cue our hands—and minds—to engage in a certain complex of motor behaviors. As such, a utensil is an ignition key for mindless eating. Take the utility out of utensils to inconvenience your mind and leverage more presence. Experiment with using either "wrong" or unfamiliar utensils to appreciate the effect of this strategy on the staying power of mindful presence. For example, use a fork to eat soup or, yes, a knife to eat peas. If you aren't familiar with using chopsticks, try eating with them. Another option would be eating with your hands. Or try makeshift utensils, perhaps a piece of celery as a spoon. Throw your mind a curveball to keep it on its toes while it eats.

Try This: Adopt a Different Posture While Eating

Another avenue to increased mindfulness is experimenting with different postures while eating. If you typically eat at a table, try sitting on the floor. Note how this change in posture changes your eating experience. Chances are, you usually sit while eating, so try eating while standing up. This will keep your mind from falling asleep over your plate and also help you notice the food.

Try This: Eat with Your Eyes Closed

Close your eyes to see—with the mind's eye of mindfulness—what you are eating. Mindfulness is "super-vision": it sees and "over-sees" with the eyes shut. Try this out in the weeks to come to keep your mind on track while you eat.

Try This: Eat in a Different Setting

Places teem with stimuli. They become conditioned cues for behavior. Redraw the map of your eating geography. Move to a different side of the table. Eat at a different table to enjoy a different view, including a different view into yourself. Eat in a different room to make room for your mind. In short, change your eating habitat to change your eating habits.

Try This: Experiment with Exotic Foods

Change up what you actually eat. Trying out unfamiliar, exotic foods will help your mind stay put on eating. The tongue is a thrill seeker; it wants an adventure. But without the tour guide of mindfulness, the tongue will miss out on the gustatory scenery. Therefore, I encourage you to combine new foods with the pattern-interruption techniques above to leverage the mindful presence you bring to eating. This will help you notice these new worlds of taste on your eating journey.

Finding the Flavor of the Moment

There are two ways of looking at flavor. One is to see flavor technically, as a convergence of taste, smell, and texture. The other take on flavor is more existential. By all means notice the flavor of the food in the technical sense, but also notice the flavor of the eating moment. Time hides itself; it slips away when unattended. It takes presence of mind to experience a moment in time. Ask yourself, "What is significant about this eating moment?" But try not to sink too deeply into this thought; try not to let your mind soar too far aloft. Just open up to the significance, if any, and let go.

Allow yourself to be aware of the irrelevancies of the eating moment. Take them in and note them, but avoid pondering them or considering them to be any deeper than they are. Here you are, Earth yourself, eating Earth, while Earth itself is spinning along on its cosmic ride— the significance of the moment need not be much more than that. Be at home in the moment, mixing mouthfuls and mindfuls

Ask yourself, "What is the flavor of this moment?" At a minimum, if you are mindful you are in touch with reality, touching the world by eating it, being touched by it as the food massages its way inside you, feeling touched by all that lived, breathed, worked, and died for you to have this eating moment. You are touched by all of this but not overwhelmed. No undue sentimentality is required. Simply eat—just eating quietly and gracefully, with awareness. Note the significance, but don't cling to it. Feel subtle awe of this life process without being paralyzed or taken aback by these invisible connections that unite us all in the triviality and momentousness of eating.

Find the moment-specific poignancy of this experience and let it pass. In searching for this flavor, release any expectations. It need not be existentially jalapeño. A plain vanilla moment would do just fine.

Practice Just Noticing

Mindfulness involves two essential mechanisms: applying a certain kind of attention and practicing disidentification. Attention can be active or passive: that of an active observer or that of an uninvolved witness. This distinction is easy to understand through contrasting such verbs as "to look" versus "to see." "To look" implies an active visual scanning, a kind of goal-oriented visual activity. "To see" implies nothing other than a fact of visual registration. Say I lost my house keys. I would have to look for them. But in the process of looking for my house keys, I might also happen to see an old concert ticket. Mindfulness is about seeing, not looking. It is about just noticing or just witnessing without attachment to or identification with what is being noticed and witnessed. This is where disidentification comes in.

Cravings (for dessert or something specific to eat, or just to keep eating) come and go. Mindfulness—as a meditative stance—allows you to recognize that craving is a transient, fleeting state of mind, and just one part of your overall experience. Mindfulness teaches you to realize that this impulse to keep on eating is but a thought inside the mind. Yes, it's part of you, but it isn't all of you—which is exactly why you can just notice it, just see it without having to stare at it. In sum, mindfulness—as a form of impulse control—is a strategy of controlling by letting go of control.

Mindfulness of Fullness

Mindful eating is a subtle balance between enjoying yourself and not getting too carried away by the undertow of this enjoyment. Keep your mind on a tether of its body: stay progressively more attuned to the emerging sensations of fullness. Make use of the fullness-sensitization training built into the first course of relaxation. Even before you started eating, you already had a chance to note the pleasant distention of your stomach as you filled up on air and water, setting that as a kind of fullness cue to watch for. So as your mind sails through the third course of actual eating, keep your attention anchored to the dynamics of your tummy.

The bigger issue is not awareness of fullness per se but your willingness to make use of this information. This will help you consciously deal with the desire to keep eating when you're already full. Mindfulness definitely comes to the rescue here. The following techniques are a few ways you can combine breath-focused relaxation with mindfulness to help yourself stop eating.

Try This: Rest in Fullness

Get a piece of paper and a pen, then trigger an impulse to eat. Think about some food you like or, better yet, expose yourself to it directly, putting that food right in front of you. Next, put on your mindfulness cap and notice cravings and thoughts of desire as they arise. Each and every time you notice a craving thought, draw a small dot on the piece of paper. Then refocus on your breathing. Do this for a few minutes.

Now take a look at your drawing. It's a series of dots—and a series of spaces. Each dot represents a craving, an impulse to eat that you registered on the radar of your awareness.

Now let's apply this to fullness. Next time you eat, have a piece of paper and pen at hand and watch for the onset of fullness. Once you feel full, sit back and notice if you have a desire to keep eating. If you do, sit it out for a few minutes while you watch your mind. Each and every time you have a desire to keep eating, draw a small dot on the piece of paper, refocus on the sensations of your breathing, and rest in the fullness of the moment. After spending a few minutes doing this, make a conscious choice about whether you'll continue eating or not.

An important note: What you decide is irrelevant at this point. What matters is that you practice mindfully pausing after the onset of a pleasant sensation of fullness.

Try This: Pause in Midmeal

As you're eating your meals in the coming weeks, occasionally stop eating and put your utensils down. Wait for your stomach to say, "Hey, aren't you going to finish the food on your plate?" Notice the body's knock on the mind's door. Recognize that this is just a fleeting impulse to continue. Whenever you feel the desire to keep eating, tap a finger on the table. You don't have to fear this impulse to keep eating. You can satisfy this impulse in a moment, but for now let it pass. It's good to practice this early in the meal, when you aren't as full and the desire to keep eating is stronger. This will help you get better at resisting the temptation to keep eating when your stomach is already pleasantly full.

Practice: Creating an Evolving Ritual

In building a ritual of mindful eating, part of the ritual is to deritualize the process of eating. In the three-course new meal of relaxation, meditation, and mindful eating, it's a good idea to ritualize the first two courses: relaxation and meditation. But do leave yourself a degree of freedom when it comes to actual eating. Recall that the point of choice awareness and pattern interruption is to get in the way of eating rituals and thereby keep the mind alert and awake while you're eating.

Let the eating part of the new meal be an evolving process of experimentation. During some meals you might keep yourself mentally awake by using your nondominant hand. During other meals you might keep your mind from falling asleep by using atypical utensils. The point is to develop a habit of breaking habits. Consider this a ritual-breaking ritual! Keep thwarting your eating habits to keep eating mindfully.

Conclusion: Ready to Ritualize?

You now have a full-fledged, total bodymind self-care ritual that is welded into the very platform of your day-to-day eating:

1. First course: Relaxation

2. Second course: Meditation

3. Third course: Eating mindfully

This three-course meal allows you to reconnect with your body, reconnect with your mind and sense of self, and reconnect with the world at large through more conscious and attuned eating. We've covered all the basics here. All that's left is to practice. But unlike other projects of skill acquisition, this one doesn't require anything fundamentally new of you. You don't have to set aside any separate time for this. Whatever else you do on any given day, you will almost assuredly be eating. The new meal approach is simply an opportunity for you to transform this daily activity—which is underutilized at best, and chronically dissatisfying at worst—into nothing less than the yoga of eating. Savor your new meal and its convergence of relaxing lungfuls, soothing nosefuls, humful mmm-fuls, soulful self-fuls, and mindful mouthfuls. That ought to fill you up!

An Amuse-Bouche of Pattern Interruption

Guess what time it is! It's time to dump a bucket of pattern-interruption ice on the eating zombie. It's time to jolt yourself awake into unmediated presence. It's time to contemplate the bottomless mystery of eating with a dose of philosophical provocation.

Gut Check, Identity Check

There are 75 trillion cells in your body. There are 750 trillion bacteria in your gut (Levy 2004). Within "your own body," your own cells are outnumbered by at least a ten-to-one ratio. Now you see why I used quotation marks around "your own body." So who are you, eater?

Eating Is Life Giving

When you eat a fruit, such as an apple, you are stepping—wittingly or unwittingly—into someone else's reproductive cycle, becoming involved in a kind of ménage à trois with a tree and Earth in a life-giving project. In fact, when you eat a piece of fruit, you are literally eating a plant-based sex organ. A fruit, botanically speaking, is a sexually active part of a flowering plant. When you consume an apple, you eat its fleshy, sweet, pulpy ovary tissue, and then you participate in the process of seed dispersal by throwing out the apple core. Naturally, if you shred the apple core and its seeds in a kitchen garbage disposal, there isn't any life-giving going on. But if you eat an apple and toss the core into your backyard, you might just be participating in the birth of a future apple tree. Ponder this apple bite from the tree of knowledge before your next meal.

Life in a Leaf

What is a leaf? According to early twentieth-century Russian scientist Konstantin Merezhkovsky (as paraphrased by Rob Dunn), "The pale green chloroplasts in plant cells evolved from bacteria ingested by plant ancestors… The green of forests was not plant matter at all,…but instead the ancient cyanobacteria held up by trees in every leaf, like so many guests standing in the window of a house, candles in their hands" (Dunn 2009, 144). Merezhkovsky's views of life-forms as composites were echoed later in the century by such American biologists as Ivan Wallin and Lynn Margulis. According to the theory of symbiogenesis, or evolution by mergers of organisms, "Key organs of eukaryote cells (mitochondria, chloroplasts, flagella, cilia, and centrioles) had their origins in ancient bacteria engulfed by another cell" (Dunn 2009, 142). My point is this: each leaf is not just a being; it is a microcosmos. Even a cabbage leaf—even if separated from the head of cabbage—is alive. So when you have a chance, eat a leaf of spinach and swallow an invisible world!

Eating Is Life Taking

Eating isn't just life giving. It is also life taking. To eat is to kill. This is true not just for carnivores, but for vegetarians and vegans. Unless you are surviving on carrion or fruit fallen from the tree, there's a good chance that something living had to die—purposefully or accidentally—to become your food.

The argument that a carrot doesn't suffer when pulled out of the ground whereas a lobster does when boiled alive is speciesism—a subjective value judgment and an arbitrary assignment of importance to particular species of life. Sure, it's easier for us humans to relate to being boiled alive than to being yanked out of the ground. Being rootless, we have no reference point for the latter. But, fundamentally, anything that is alive wants to live. If we eat a living thing, we kill it. So there are no saints among animals. Animals—whether the lion or the lamb—kill to eat and live, whereas plants photosynthesize to live. Even an ascetic vegan surviving on a handful of uncooked fruits and nuts is still predatory upon plant life. So let us eat, as we must, but not with guilt—rather, with grateful humility.

Primordial Cooking

Which came first, swallowing or digestion? If you said swallowing, you're in for a surprise. When prokaryotes—our earliest ancestors (who still inhabit Earth in the guise of bacteria)—first evolved, they were basically living stomachs floating freely in the primordial ocean. Prokaryotes accomplish digestion outside their cell membranes by surrounding themselves with "a kind of halo of digestive enzymes" (Stewart 1998, 78). Prokaryotes digest first and then swallow. Now digest this: When you cook, are you not predigesting (preprocessing) that which you are yet to swallow? Case in point: Which takes less work to chew, a boiled carrot or a raw one? In a sense, your stomach is an anatomically internalized kitchen.

Eating Outcasts

Breaking bread with someone is a form of intimacy. But eating can also alienate. As Lucille Schulberg wrote in *Historic India*, "A primary impulse behind the caste system was probably the fear of spiritual pollution through food" (1968, 140):

[The Indians believed that] the *mana*, or 'soul-stuff' of human beings was the same as the soul-stuff of food, especially vegetable food. Unbroken cereal food—grasses growing in a field, seeds waiting to be gathered—retained their soul-stuff when they were handled; anyone could touch and eat them safely. But once grain was softened in cooking or seeds were pressed for their oil, their soul-stuff mixed with the soul-stuff of the person who prepared the food... A taboo on sharing food with an outsider—that is, with anyone not in [one's] own caste—was a protective measure against such spiritual pollution... The higher a caste, the more restricted its menu.

A couple of questions for you. Do you believe that the "soul-stuff" of food is the same as your "soul-stuff"? If you do, how does this inform your eating? If you don't, how does that influence your eating practices? Also, in what ways are you an eating outcast? How does your eating style isolate you? Ponder how *what* you eat might have stratified you socially.

A Seed of Awareness

Botanically, a seed is not the potential for life; it's already a life—a tiny plant life with a lunch box of its own food, awaiting a journey of life. In my book *The Lotus Effect* (2010), I shared a story about 1,300-year-old lotus seeds that managed to germinate and grow when given a chance. Eat a handful of seeds to meditate on how innocently your metabolic needs result in killing. Here you are, taking care of yourself and, at the same time, denying a living thing its chance to grow and flourish. Wrestle for a moment with the question of which is more important, you or those seeds. My answer is you, of course. If those seeds could eat you to survive, they would. Life is inevitably self-serving. As long as there is a self, it is going to serve itself a serving of environment. That's just how it is. So, even as you contemplate this inevitable zero-sum metabolic scenario, enjoy your sustenance. No guilt, I say— just compassion and gratitude!

Eating Kills

Life is movement. Movement creates friction, damage, and erosion. Eating, as part of this process of living, is no exception.

Eating kills—and it kills the eater. How? Through choking, toxicity, free radicals, and countless forms of metabolic wear and tear. Studies of calorie-restriction diets uniformly show that eating less leads to decreased morbidity and mortality (Walford 2000)—up to a point. Of course, no food means no metabolism means no life. However, too much food means too much metabolic wear and tear means premature death. So ponder the irony that the very food that allows you to live also hastens your demise, even if you're eating goji berries, with their renowned antioxidant properties. Any eating event is an instance of metabolic wear and tear. Life is its own opportunity and its own risk. Strangely enough, life kills itself. Life is messing with us, playing with us. Since this is inevitable, let's choose to laugh at this peculiar paradox of arising and ceasing, at this peculiar wave of creation and destruction.

Share your mindful eating experiences online using the Mindful Eating Tracker at http://www.eatingthemoment.com/mindfulness-tracker.

chapter 5

Reclaiming the Calorie

Linguistic habits can institutionalize and enforce an overly static vision of the world.

— Roger Ames and David Hall,
Dao De Jing: A Philosophical Translation

The human mind runs on language. As Western civilization careens toward obesity, it has become caught up in calorie counting in part because it has gotten fixated on a particular meaning of the word "calorie." The word "calorie" has become a nutritional bugaboo. We've come to see calories as a horde of menacing ghouls that lurk in our food, enticing us into ever-greater nutritional sins. The goal of this chapter is to reclaim both the word "calorie" and the calorie itself.

Nutritional Calories vs. Experiential Calories

Let's begin to reconstruct your relationship with the word "calorie" by considering the distinction between a nutritional calorie and what I call an experiential calorie. A nutritional calorie is a unit of energy. The job of a nutritional calorie is to fuel your body. An experiential calorie is a unit of awareness—of conscious presence, meaning, and psychospiritual warmth. The job of an experiential calorie is to nourish and enrich your mind. A nutritional calorie can do its body-heating work without any presence of mind. An experiential calorie requires presence of mind to unlock its warmth.

Nutritionally Empty Calories vs. Existentially Empty Calories

A nutritionally empty calorie is fuel without the benefit of any micronutrients—vitamins, minerals, and so on. An existentially empty calorie is a nutritional calorie that is consumed without awareness and mindfulness. Here's an example: Say you drive a few miles to a farmers' market on Saturday (expending gas and time) and buy a pint of luscious, organically grown strawberries. Then you go home, turn on the TV, and mindlessly engulf the strawberries without noticing the subtleties of their flavor, let alone pausing to appreciate the bigger picture of this eating moment. I'd consider those nutritionally rich physical calories to be existentially empty, since they were consumed without any awareness. While your body undoubtedly benefits from those nutritionally high-quality calories, your mind hasn't been enriched. You felt no particular connection either to yourself, the eater, or to this Earth that you are eating (and becoming).

Now, let's turn this around. Say you drive to your local convenience store and pop in for a donut—definitely nutritional junk without any health benefits. Nevertheless, you decide to have a quality eating moment. You drive a few blocks to a nearby park, turn off the car engine, roll the window down to let in some breeze, and allow yourself to lean into this treat. You take your time. You notice the simple art of the donut. You smell its aroma, taste its sweetness, and feel its texture in your mouth. As you eat, you watch some kids playing in the distance and happen to recall how excited you got about donuts as a child. You stop after a few bites and notice some pigeons nearby, scavenging around a picnic table. You decide to share your moment of eating bliss. You get out of your car, break up the rest of the donut into crumbs, and scatter them around. Then you go home.

This is an existential highlight. Sure, from the standpoint of your body you ate a bunch of nutritionally empty calories, but experientially and existentially you have enriched yourself, connecting with yourself and with the world at large. You managed to turn shit into gold by converting nutritionally empty calories into existential fullness. Good for you. And that isn't just good for your mind; it's good for your body too, because what's good for the mind tends to also be good for the body. After all, these two words ("body" and "mind") are describing one and the same whole. Of course, if you had eaten that same donut mindlessly, you would have missed an opportunity for self-enrichment on both fronts.

Mind-Warming Eating

In the weeks to come, after your first two courses of relaxation and mindfulness, when you begin to eat, pause between bites every now and then and ask yourself, "Experientially speaking, what am I getting out of this eating moment? How is my mind being enriched? How is my spirit, essence, or self being warmed or touched or moved by this eating moment?" This question can take on a variety of flavors, as the following sections indicate. Sample and savor all of them.

Ask Yourself: What Are the Meditational Calories of This Moment?

As you eat, pause to consider the interdependence of people, places, and events that converged into one seamless process in time in order for this meal to reach your lips. Of course, the sun didn't shine for you, the grapes didn't grow for you, the farmer didn't cultivate the grapes for

you, and the canner didn't make the grape jelly for you in particular...
And yet, somehow, as you are spreading grape jelly on your toast, you
are now the beneficiary of this endless process of transmutation and
collaboration. Alternatively, as you focus on the automaticity of your
hand-to-mouth motions—this smooth, habitual machinery—perhaps
you will awaken to both marvel at and fear the ease and pervasiveness
of this mindlessness. Or as you watch this food and this moment come
and go, perhaps you will consider the impermanence and transience of
all things, including yourself.

Ask Yourself: What Are the Ethical Calories of This Moment?

Ethics, not politics, are the foundation of effective citizenship. Ethics
are personalized priorities, or values. Politics is just the public expression of these priorities. So ask yourself, "How am I expressing my values
in this moment? Are my eating choices an accurate reflection of what I
stand for ethically? Is there any dissonance between what I eat and my
values? Is there any dissonance between how I eat and my values? Is
anything eating at me as I'm eating? Or am I eating with a clean
conscience?"

Ask Yourself: What Are the Aesthetic Calories of This Moment?

The Armenian-Russian mystic George Gurdjieff used to talk about the
sensory hunger we experience because of our generally mindless and
unaware mode of living. He believed that the mind literally hungers for
sensation. So satisfy it. Ask yourself, "Am I allowing myself to notice
the humble, unpretentious beauty of what I'm about to eat? Am I taking
in the aesthetics of the setting? Is there any nature to notice? Is the
ambience of the place congruent with my mood? In short, am I taking
in the beauty of the moment?"

Ask Yourself: What Are the Hedonic Calories of This Moment?

With the term "hedonic calories," I'm not talking about unbridled hedonism. In terms of food, hedonics are about foodgasms, not food orgies. Ask yourself, "Am I enjoying this eating moment, this moment of living? Am I sensing, tasting, and savoring, or am I just shoveling down that which just moments ago I so carefully cooked or so meticulously selected off the menu? Am I noticing the dynamic art of food, the polysensory drama of the flavor as the aroma, taste, and texture blended into one experiential focus? Am I having fun?"

Ask Yourself: What Are the Existential Calories of This Moment?

To exist (psychologically, not just physically) is to stand out, that is, to distinguish self from environment. Ask yourself, "Am I...here? Am I... present? Am I...aware of myself? Will I remember myself having this moment, or will it go unnoticed?" Pull yourself out of oblivion. See your self. Stand out to your own eyes. If this sounds a bit circular and confusing, that's because it is confusing. Here too, you are a trinity of sorts: the seer, the seen, and the act of seeing. Be the object of your own subjectivity: notice you noticing you. Practice existentially outstanding eating.

Ask Yourself: What Are the Social Calories of This Moment?

Eating connects us with others and disconnects as well. Ask yourself, "Who am I with and why? Am I eating because they're hungry? Are they eating because I'm hungry? Are we eating because we're hungry for food, or are we eating because we're hungry for connection? Or are we just randomly in this moment, with the food in front of us perhaps being the only social common denominator?"

Conclusion: Meaning Is Caloric

In this chapter I set out to rehabilitate the word "calorie," which Western culture has largely (literally!) come to view as a kind of nutritional enemy of the body-state. I've attempted to broaden the meaning of the word "calorie" from body-talk to mind-talk. An experiential calorie—whether aesthetic or social, ethical or existential, meditational or hedonic—is a calorie that awakens the mind to the meaning of the moment. Meaning is informationally caloric. Meaning enriches. Meaning energizes, mobilizes, and fires us up. Thus, meaning is heat, and information is calories for the mind. That's why we, the information hunter-gatherers, search for meaning and binge on information. So if you're feeling a bit meaning hungry, look no further than your next meal. Recognize that mind food *is* body food. After all, as I've emphasized, these two words, "mind" and "body," are but two sides of one and the same organismic coin.

Any quest is a question. Certainty initiates no adventures. Whereas mindless eating takes your mind nowhere special, mindful eating is an open-ended inquiry into the mystery of what is. Reclaiming the word "calorie" is part of this quest. In the old-school (current Western) view, calories are void of existential meaning. Like money, they are something to count and not overspend. The new meal view encourages you to go ahead and blow your existential wad. It prompts you to spend your mind and not save your presence until some later moment in time (which, by the way, will never occur, because life is always now). Rethink the word "calorie" and see it as a quest for existential-experiential warmth. Ask yourself, "What is this eating moment about?" And then take in the calories of the moment.

chapter 6

Reinventing the
Oryoki Meal

Knowing when enough is enough is really satisfying.

— *Dao De Jing*

A meal is an event. Eating is the process behind it. Paying attention to the process of eating is both self-fulfilling and self-emptying. As such, a meal that involves focus on the process is not just a nutritional event but also a meditative event. Buddhists have long understood this. Let's learn from them—in essence, but not necessarily in form.

Oryoki Form

Oryoki, which is Japanese for "just enough," is a form of eating meditation—a highly choreographed, protocol-driven practice that follows a strict procession of cues to keep the mind focused on the process of eating. On the technical side, an *oryoki* meal involves a set of nested wooden bowls (*jihatsu*), with the largest bowl (*zuhatsu*) being called the

Buddha bowl, and a set of eating utensils that are wrapped up, burrito-style, into a cloth. *Oryoki* has built-in pauses for chanting prayer and expressing grace or gratitude, and a formal opportunity for the donation of leftovers. *Oryoki* is a great example of a total reinvention of the meal! This ancient tradition is still alive and well in some circles. It's still practiced in Zen monasteries and some Buddhist retreat centers.

Converting the Dining Hall into a Meditation Hall

Why did the *oryoki* meal evolve? Here are a few lay speculations of mine: Imagine yourself as a medieval Zen master charged with managing a Buddhist monastery. Day in, day out, you get a bunch of folks banging on your door seeking admission, refuge, protection—in other words, room and board. Unable to read minds and screen out dharma bums from sincerely motivated seekers, you come up with a brilliant scheme. You decide to turn the dining hall into a meditation hall. You come up with a highly codified eating protocol that emphasizes a precise sequence of movements that includes stopping when one is full, cleaning up after oneself, and liturgical chanting. This brilliant administrative solution kills several birds with one stone. First, you've got a captive audience: a hungry stomach means an attentive mind. Second, insisting on mindful consumption ensures that monks don't mindlessly overeat, which helps ensure that monastery food supplies are appropriately utilized. Third, by instituting a carefully choreographed, synchronized eating ritual, you're making sure that the ragtag team of bodies that walked in the door acts as a mindfully united community; that the novices who still overvalue their egos have their egos repeatedly challenged at each meal by being told how to eat; and that there isn't much of a mess in the mess hall when everyone has finished eating.

Seriously though, these administrative and hazing motivations aside, the *oryoki* meal is an attempt to turn eating into a platform for meditation. Doing so ensures a seamless integration of meditation into the nuts and bolts of daily living. *Oryoki*—in its essence—is *zazen* (a form of sitting meditation), with the main difference being that the sitting is done in the dining hall, not the meditation hall, effectively collapsing the distinction between these two spaces and merging them into one: a field of practice for mindful living. I encourage you to experiment with turning your own dining hall into a meditation hall.

Solutions Become Problems

There's a problem: ceremonies and rituals tend to calcify, like fossils. Traditions designed to keep the mind flowing become stagnant, fixed, and crystallized as form begins to eclipse essence. This is the dialectic of mindful eating: the more you focus your mind, the more you potentially close it.

Furthermore, from a layperson's perspective, an *oryoki* meal is time-consuming and, frankly, a flat-out hassle. Yes, it's a profound choreography of body and mind and an exotic peak experience. But as I see it, in its strict, classic form, an *oryoki* meal is utterly impractical in day-to-day living. Sure, you can attend a Zen retreat and spend a week or two learning how to eat in orchestrated silence. But we can't stay in a mind spa forever. At some point we have to reenter our lives. The challenge is to import the attitude of *oryoki* into day-to-day eating without having to go on a full-blown sabbatical at every meal.

Try This: Ask Yourself What a Mind Needs to Be Fed

The word *oryoki* is composed of three symbols: ō, the receiver's attitude of acceptance in response to whatever food is offered; *ryō*, a measure, or an amount, to be received; and *ki*, the bowl. Together, these three syllables add up to just enough satisfaction. Indeed, what does a body need to be fed? It needs food that the mind accepts—that the mind doesn't mind, if you will; a certain amount of it—a meal or measure of it (indeed, the word "meal" stems from the Latin word for "measure"); and a way to hold the food—a bowl or other container. Now ask yourself, "What does a mind need to be fed?" Mull this over when you have a chance.

Zen Essence, Zen Form

The *oryoki* meal is a highly prescribed form of eating. But its essence isn't the meditative decor of eating. The essence of *oryoki* is the essence of eating. And what is the essence of eating? Filling up a void. Consider a monk who eats *oryoki*-style. Take him out of his orange robe and put him in a pair of jeans and a T-shirt. Take away his bowl and give him a paper plate. Take away his chopsticks and give him a spork. Then watch him eat. While the props have changed, his mindfulness of eating hasn't. Mindful eating is mindful eating, independent of form. Even sitting is irrelevant. Take this eating *zazen* and morph it into *kinhin* (a form of walking meditation), and it's still an eating meditation. Have this Zen monk walk and eat a take-out container full of deep-fried potato skins while dressed in a tuxedo. As long as his mind is full of the experience of eating, it matters not whether he is sitting or walking, or whether he's eating rice out of a lacquered wooden bowl or having a frozen chocolate-covered banana on a stick. My point? The "just enough" meme of *oryoki* is this: just eating is plenty enough.

But it's all too easy to miss this with the distraction of the esoteric accoutrements of the *oryoki* form. Form stands out; it appeals to the eye. We get confused by the understated glamour of this formal tradition. We get hung up on the irrelevancies of the context. The human mind is a junkie for form. We eagerly exchange essence for form with cars, with fashion, and with relationships. Mindfulness is the antidote. Form passes and essence remains. As a form of eating, *oryoki* matters only to the extent that it draws the mind to the essence of eating. A mindlessly performed *oryoki* meal isn't *oryoki* even if it looks like it is. By the same token, mindfully consuming a slice of pizza while you sit at a bus stop, just eating, just may be *oryoki* enough.

Oryoki Lite

Here's what I propose: *oryoki* lite. *Oryoki* lite doesn't require a specialized set of bowls. A paper plate will suffice. It doesn't call for sitting in a half lotus on the floor. A chair at your regular dining table will do just fine. It isn't about following the protocol. In fact, it's about breaking the protocol. It's about waking yourself up with something as simple as using your nondominant hand to eat or using unfamiliar utensils to throw your eating kinesthetics off balance and wake up your mind. *Oryoki* lite doesn't require knowledge of liturgical chants. A simple mmm-mantra of savoring between mindful bites will do.

Oryoki lite isn't about Buddhist form; it's about Buddhist essence— simply waking yourself up without any need for exotic Buddhist fanfare. After all, that's what the word "Buddha" means: the one who is awake— not the one in an orange robe with a set of begging bowls and a mantra in his or her mouth, but anyone, including you or me, being intermittently, if only briefly, present in our lives. Full-time presence isn't required. That's for monks. Perhaps one mindful eating moment per meal will suffice. That kind of *oryoki* meal, as I see it, is indeed *just enough*.

Practice: Experiencing Oryoki Lite

In the weeks to come, after a first course of relaxation and a second course of meditation, have an *oryoki* lite meal. Turn off the TV, put the paper away, and just eat, following whatever process or protocol you like. Does this surprise you? You may ask, "Is this it? Isn't there anything more to this exercise?" Nope. Just eat. Practice *oryoki* essence and let go of *oryoki* form. That's more than enough.

Try This: Play with a Buddha Bowl

Having dispensed with *oryoki* formalities, let's reintroduce one of them, allowing the pendulum of reinvention to swing back a bit. This will be delightfully simple. If you don't already have a wooden bowl, buy one and use it for all of your meals for the next week. Yes, you might have to wash it between the main dish and dessert. Welcome this sudden pattern break. As you rinse the bowl, reempty your mind with the question "Am I still hungry, or am I just following the old meal sequence of courses?"

This is actually a value-added experiment. Be sure that your bowl isn't dishwasher safe. This allows you to work with a key pattern-interruption strategy wherein inconvenience is a meditative opportunity. Having to hand wash your Buddha bowl before or after you eat is part of the mindful eating mind-set. Is this a hassle? You bet it is—but what a potentially contemplative hassle! Find the opportunity to be a bit of a monk in this monkey wrench of an inconvenience.

I predict that with time you will come to appreciate the habit-forming continuity of eating from one and the same bowl. The familiar emptiness of your Buddha bowl before you fill it up with food will serve as a cue to empty your mind before you eat. So get a bowl and be a bowl.

Conclusion: Mind on a Paper Plate

Philosopher and public speaker Jiddu Krishnamurti once issued the following caution: "Both collective and individual rituals give a certain quietness to the mind; they offer a vital contrast to the everyday, humdrum life. There is a certain amount of beauty and orderliness in ceremonies, but fundamentally...they soon dull the mind and heart" (2006, 19). The point is, you don't need an *oryoki*-style bowl. You don't need chopsticks. You don't need to sit in a lotus position on the floor. You don't even necessarily need to stay silent. The esoteric idiosyncrasies of this exotic ancient eating ritual are, as I see it, irrelevant to its essence. What matters is simply this: when you eat, just eat. So grab a paper plate and let your mind feast.

An Amuse-Bouche of Pattern Interruption

We wash dishes. We brush our teeth. How about some mental hygiene? Yes, it's that time again—time to empty your mind, time to sweep out the cobwebs of preconceived notions about eating, time for self-renewing pattern interruption. Forgot how this works? No problem. Let me remind you: open your mind to a new perspective on eating so that you can refresh your eating style.

Bodymind Yo-Yo

We are not just *what* we eat; we are also *how* we eat. If we eat mindlessly, to the extent to which mindless eating leads to overeating, our bodies expand and our minds shrink—experientially, of course, not literally. When we eat mindlessly, we miss out on the experience of that eating moment of life as it passes by. If, however, we eat mindfully, to the extent to which mindful eating curbs overeating and assists weight loss, our bodies shrink and our minds expand. We don't go up a hat size, but our conscious event horizon widens and our view becomes more spacious and inclusive. We grow existentially and feel enriched experientially. We come back to life. We come back online. Open your mind to open your view before you open your mouth. Remember, a living tube must stay open to the flow.

Own Your Dependence

There is no you without the environment, no ego without the eco. There has never been a life in a total and absolute vacuum. Face this fact: you are fully and completely dependent on all that's around you. Eating is there to remind you of this dependence, of this interconnectedness. Next time you sit down to eat, consciously own this dependence. Yes, you do depend on this lowly green pea on your plate, on this bite of apple, on this slice of bread, and on this glass of water. As your chin dips down toward food, turn this forward leaning toward a bow of gratitude—and a bow to yourself. There is no you without this food. This lowly green pea, this bite of apple, this slice of bread, this glass of water is about to become you. Turn your forward leaning toward your meal into a deep bow of a greeting: "Here I come. I am this."

Eating Is Self-Synchronization

Eating is metabolic self-care. As such, eating teaches us the difference between aloneness and being lonely. Eating alone is an opportunity for solitude. Eat a few meals by yourself and without distractions: no TV, no smartphone, no paper, no music—just you, having your own company for dessert. See what unfolds.

Mindful Food Partnership

In his book *Sun of gOd*, Gregory Sams encourages readers to be mindful of their relationship to the food they eat: "Look at your food, taste it, feel it, and feel for it." Then he asks, "Do you want it to become you?" (2009, 213). What a question! Mindful eating is mindful partnership. In eating, we enter into a union with what is, wedding an aspect of reality and entering into a marriage with matter. So it makes great sense to be selective, to be choosy, discriminative, and mindful about what we allow to enter into us, about what we allow ourselves to become. We are what we eat, and we are the company we keep. So as you enter into a communion with reality at your next meal, take a good look at your prospective partner. Who will make you a better partner in health? Who deserves the ring of your metabolic commitment: this lifeless deep-fried chicken finger or this ruddy carrot stick? Do you want to partner up with this food, or will you seek to divorce it with another diet following the fleeting honeymoon of taste? Will this food be a partner for life and health, or just another nutritionally and existentially meaningless one-night stand of unhealthy eating? Choose a lover that loves you back, a food that nourishes and supports you, rather than choosing nutritionally and experientially empty calories that you'll end up having to support with your health insurance premiums.

Rock-Eating Rock

Take a look at your pearly whites and chew on this: human teeth are "converted toxic waste dumps: evolutionarily, [they] derive from the need of marine cells to dump calcium waste outside their cell membranes" (Sagan 1990, 63). Next time you have a calcium-rich glass of milk or heap of kale, consider the irony of this eating moment: made, in part, of rock, you are eating part rock. What a mouthful of stones this Earth is. This third rock from the sun is grinding and gnashing itself through you. How marvelous!

Eating Is Self-Transcendence

You are an eating pyramid: billions of micromouths with your macromouth on top. Your eating—within the confines of your body—is communal. With this in mind, ask yourself who eats. Asking yourself, "Who is eating?" is really just a way of asking, "Who am I?" Indeed, who are you, composite creature? Chew on this mystery of eating as "you" eat. Transcend your stereotypes of yourself.

Two Kinds of "Just Eating"

Eating can mean so many different things. It can be a proclamation of ethics, a form of emotional and physical self-care, or a pretext to socialize. But then there is just eating: eating for its own sake. This kind of "just eating" can be either mindful or mindless. We can mindlessly graze on and on and on until a concerned significant other asks, "What are you doing?" Perhaps defensively, we might reply, "Nothing much. Just eating." But "just eating" can also be of a mindful kind—when you kill the TV, put away your smartphone, and *just eat*. As you plan to eat today, ponder which form of "just eating" will do true justice to your eating intentions: the mindless kind or the mindful kind.

Eating Isn't "Just Eating"

Most people see meditation as an extra thing to do. But many activities, eating included, can serve as a platform for meditation, and with eating this is invaluable. As you eat your next meal, don't just have a mouthful—have a mindful. What's a mindful? A moment of conscious eating. Don't just feast on food, feast on the moment. Remind yourself that eating isn't "just eating." Turn your dining hall into a meditation hall. Recognize that eating isn't just an opportunity to open your mouth, but also an opportunity to open your mind. Open wide!

Share your mindful eating experiences online using the Mindful Eating Tracker at http://www.eatingthemoment.com/mindfulness-tracker.

chapter 7

Reinventing the Dessert

Kenge [the Pygmy] was all alone, dancing around and singing softly to himself as he gazed up at the tree tops... I came to the clearing and asked, jokingly, why he was dancing alone... "But I am not dancing alone," he said. "I am dancing with the forest, dancing with the moon." Then, with the utmost unconcern, he ignored me and continued his dance of love and life.

— Colin Turnbull, *The Forest People*

Dessert is entertainment for an empty mind with an already full stomach. There was a time when there was no need for dessert. Eating was about survival. Surviving was entertainment enough. Then we got civilized. We settled down and got good at agriculture and food storage. We learned how to make sure we always had enough to eat to survive. Once survival became assured, merely eating was no longer stimulating enough. We had to come up with something new. We had to find something exotic, some hard-to-get foodstuffs to provoke the mind. We had to spice things up to make eating stimulating and interesting again. Just eating became boring, and we had to do something about this eating boredom. We yearned for subtleties ("subtleties" being a term for "dessert" in medieval England). We yearned to rekindle the sense of eating enjoyment. And we found it in dessert, in a stand-alone meal-within-a-meal (known as *secundae mensa*, meaning "second meal," in Roman times). The goal of this chapter is to rediscover the dessert available in every bite.

Mindful Eating Koan

I'm sure you've heard that classic Zen koan "If a tree falls in a forest and no one is there to hear it, does it make a sound?" Of course it does, and, of course, it doesn't. It depends on what you mean by "sound." If you mean air waves, then of course the tree makes a sound, whether it falls in the middle of a concert hall or on the surface of the moon. But if by "sound" you mean perception of sound—the subjective experience of hearing when air waves knock on the doors of the eardrums—then no, a tree that falls makes no sound if there are no ears to hear those air waves.

With this in mind, consider the following question: If food is eaten mindlessly, does it have a taste? Of course it does, and, of course, it doesn't. If by "taste" you mean objective chemical properties (this much salt, that much sugar, and so on), then yes, food has a taste even if you feed it to a robot. But if by "taste" you mean the perception of taste, the subjective registering of the flavor, then no, food doesn't have any taste if eaten mindlessly. If we are mindlessly busy watching TV or surfing the Internet, we are blind and deaf to the taste of the food we are eating.

Now let me ask you this: Is ice cream a dessert? Of course it is, and, of course, it isn't. If it's eaten mindfully, it is. But if it's inhaled unattended by the mind, it isn't.

Now, my final koan for you: Is a pickle a dessert?

Every Meal Is a Dessert

In essence, dessert is a treat for the mind. In the old-school meal it is perhaps the most mindfully eaten course—the one that's actively anticipated and energetically enjoyed. The psychology of dessert is literally to please the mind, to create an experience of gustatory enjoyment. As such, dessert is a course of pleasure. The new meal paradigm doesn't rely on sweetness to evoke pleasure; rather, it uses mindfulness to leverage pleasure, no matter what you're eating. As such, each meal can be viewed as a nonstop dessert, a continuous experience of eating pleasure, facilitated not through taste but through attending to taste. Indeed, a mindlessly eaten classic dessert has no taste, just as a tree that falls in a forest with no one there to hear it makes no sound. Without presence of mind there is no experience, no matter what you're eating. Conversely, presence of mind turns any decent meal into a potential moment of delight. Mindfulness is the best pastry chef.

Dessert = Pleasure

Historically, dessert was synonymous with sweetness. Modern-day desserts, however, are less about sweetness and more about subtlety, uniqueness, presentation. And for some folks, the treat course of the meal might be anything but sweet. It might be a handful of salty nuts or wasabi peas. The idea of the dessert has been undergoing a gradual but inevitable distillation. At its core, dessert is not about the specifics of the taste but about pleasure. Equating dessert with pleasure is an important point in the evolution of mindful eating, and one that makes every dish a potential dessert. After all, mindful eating is fundamentally hedonic; it's about savoring and rediscovering the pleasure of eating in every bite.

Mindfulness = Pleasure

Let's face it: we don't buy what we don't plan to enjoy. When you shop for food, everything you put in your cart is prescreened for potential pleasure. Therefore, everything you buy is potentially a dessert, that is, a potential source of pleasure. At least in the West, we have reached a point where we expect that everything we eat should taste good. But then, all too often, we mindlessly tune out and ignore the taste of the very thing we set out to enjoy. So we miss out on pleasure.

Mindfulness to the rescue! Mindfulness is a kind of culinary alchemy that can experientially elevate a bowl of brown rice into a serving of tiramisu. Mindful eating is about tapping the pleasure potential of the food we so carefully selected and prepared. Jon Kabat-Zinn, a Western pioneer of mindfulness, introduced the now-iconic raisin meditation in his mindfulness-based stress reduction programs (1990). Workshop participants would be led into a moment of eating mindfulness to rediscover a foodgasm in a lowly raisin. Pleasure, and thus dessert, lies hidden beneath the surface everywhere. Mindfulness, not the tongue, is the shovel that helps dig it up.

Rethink the dessert. Recognize the pleasure potential in everything you eat. Start using the term "dessert" indiscriminately, as in "For dessert I will have some soup." Yes, it sounds a bit strange. But thinking along these lines sets an intention of enjoyment. When you tell yourself that you'll have some soup for dessert, you're reminding yourself to mindfully enjoy it. You're reminding yourself to delight your mind with yet another moment of eating.

Pleasure Is a Choice

To eat is to know. Back in the primordial days of our origins, we explored through mouth. Mouth was a hand—just like it still is for little kids, and for dogs that carry tennis balls for us to throw. Our earliest ancestors knew the world by tasting it. They would taste this and taste that to see what "this" and "that" were like, and once they found out, they would then "know the taste" and keep choosing the tastes that they liked again and again.

You have to choose to interact with what you are eating if you are to know its taste. A zombie mind makes no choices; it simply follows the well-trodden groove of habit. An eating zombie runs on a program: ignore the main course and then wake up for dessert because dessert is the thing to be enjoyed, whereas the main course is just to be eaten. Of course, the zombie mind doesn't see its own inconsistencies. It overlooks the fact that the foods it chose for the main course were chosen on the basis of anticipated pleasure. Once the zombie mind is at the table and knows there's dessert ahead, it goes on cruise control until it finally gets to that last-ditch effort to enjoy itself.

That's old-school thinking. The new meal paradigm postpones no pleasure. Choose to enjoy yourself from the very beginning. There's no need to wait until you feel too stuffed to care. Start every meal with the dessert of mindful pleasure.

Try This: Document Pleasure

The next time you sit down to eat, have a pen and piece of paper at hand and, as you eat, write a plus sign for each moment of pleasure you consciously register. If the page is conspicuously blank, ask yourself, "What is the pleasure potential of this moment?" Let go of preconceived notions about dessert and just focus on pleasure. When you arrive at the end of the meal and begin to habitually think about what you're going to have for dessert, take a look at the record of the pleasure you've already had. You might just have a brain wave: "Hey, wait a second, I've already had my dessert. I'm satisfied."

Try This: Rediscover the Dessert in a Dessert

Don't get me wrong: I'm not opposed to dessert in the classic sense. If you want a traditional dessert, then by all means treat yourself to it. Just do so mindfully—or run the risk of missing out on the pleasure. Use pattern-interruption techniques, such as eating with a nondominant hand, and sensation-enhancing strategies, such as eating with your eyes closed, to leverage maximum pleasure out of the experience.

Conclusion: A "Diet" of Desserts

In sum: mindfulness = pleasure = dessert. If you want dessert, serve yourself some mindfulness. Most of us average three meals a day. Most of these meals have at least a couple of dishes or foodstuffs to enjoy. If consumed mindfully, this adds up to at least half a dozen desserts a day. Remember, mindful eating = pleasure-based eating. Mind is its own source of pleasure. Enjoy yourself no matter what you're eating. You are your own dessert.

An Amuse-Bouche of Pattern Interruption

Mind—when made up—stops flowing. Habits, stereotypes, definitions, and preconceived notions are like nails in the coffin: they keep a lid on change and keep mind boxed in. As disorienting and confusing as pattern interruption may be, it liberates the zombie out of its casket of logic. As you gear up for another day of eating, use the pattern interruption vignettes below as the tools of conscious rebellion. It's time to let your mind out of the cage of mindless eating. Have yourself an appetizer of meditative presence.

A Serving of Timelessness

Consumer societies thrive on consumption zombies. Mindful eating is a way to end this machinery of mindlessness. Mindful eating leads to mindful living, which leads back to mindful eating, which circles back to mindful living. Reinvent your eating to reinvent your living. Mindful eating is an opportunity to wake up, typically at least three times per day. Find a clock or watch that isn't running and set it on your dining table as a metaphor, and as a reminder that eating is an opportunity for timelessness. Here you are. You made time to be here and to eat. So take your time, be here, and eat.

Oral Tradition

Just like an endless echo, the oral tradition of human eating reverberates from one generation of eating zombies to the next. Who taught you to ignore yourself as you eat? Who are you teaching to ignore Earth while eating it? What's your role in this cultural habit of mindless eating?

A Self-Remembering Self

You can't quite rely on the body to wake itself up: the sleeper is asleep. Your body is never there long enough to be counted on to reappear; it's changing from nanosecond to nanosecond, with each breath and each bite. In terms of your body, you have never been fixed and unchanging. Asking your body to remember to slow down the next time you eat is like mailing an unaddressed letter. The body you're mailing it to doesn't exist yet. The body that is yet to eat the next meal hasn't yet been born. But you—the ineffable presence of consciousness—remain from one momentary reincarnation of body to the next throughout all of your metabolic metamorphoses. Write a letter from your mind to your mind, from self to self, to remember itself—from one meal to the next—through the oral tradition of mindful eating. Practice mindful eating to cultivate a self-remembering self.

The Lila of Eating

As kids we like to role-play, pretending and testing the boundaries of our reality. We even play dead. Any game of pretense is both a learning about the world and a learning about oneself. In trying to divine what it would be like to be so-and-so or such-and-such, we figure out who we are as we notice our sameness through all the roles we play. But what is it that remains constant and immutable as we morph from one pretense to another? This question is an ancient game of knowledge, and we play it out every day when we eat. Eating is also an exchange of information, a role reversal: the eater eats food and becomes food for another eater, for no other reason than to live.

Eating is also a form of play or *lila*, a Hindu concept which is "understood to be purposeless divine activity" (Haberman 1994, 229). *Lila* is a form of cosmic drama, the game of self-perpetuating creation. It's a journey through the forest of life that transforms the traveler through an endless cycle of change for no reason other than mere play. This is a powerfully sobering and liberating proposition: that "all life is *lila*, or purposeless play" (Haberman 1994, viii). As you play the drama of eating, ask yourself, "Why am I doing this? What is the point of this eating act? Why build and maintain this body only to see it deteriorate with age?"

Plumb the seeming pointlessness of this eating transmutation: Here you are, excavating the world in search of nutrients and sustenance, and continually re-creating yourself from the reality you consume and dressing yourself up into the flesh of reality. But what for? Allow your mind to chase around in circles of self-justification. And then, when you're finally ready to stop playing the game of meaning, allow yourself to leave all these question unanswered.

People often ask, "What's the point of life?" The point of life is living. That's the *lila* of it. Eat to play. Play to eat. This is your turn, living matter—your turn at the game of creation. Build your body, build your mind, build your meaning, build your legacy, build your pyramids and empires, build this edifice of life. And enjoy the hell out of the process. Life is playtime—your playtime. It's the time for your drama, for your learning, and for your loving, and eating makes it possible. Indeed, how else will the Universe educate its own matter if not by giving it a chance to live? Life schools matter about itself through your eyes, through your mouth, and through your play. And in playing, the Universe constantly changes itself so that there is always something new to learn, discover, and understand. Play with this food for thought.

Process Is the Point

What's the point of eating? To live. What's the point of living? To eat. See the circle? Sometimes people ask, "Do you eat to live, or do you live to eat?" My answer is usually "both and neither." Notice the circle disappear.

As you eat your next meal, ask yourself, "What is the point of all this?"

Then consider this: life is a process, not a point. To reduce the process of life to a point is artificial. Of course, we could play word games in which we say something along the lines of "Process *is* the point," often encapsulated in phrases like "The journey is the destination."

So, as you eat your next meal, restate the question: "What is the *process* of all this?"

Notice what changes when you shift from "What is the point of all this?" to "What is the process of all this?" Notice which question closes doors and which opens doors.

Ponder this meal-wheel, this perpetual carousel of eating and living. Eating Earth we become Earth. Is that pointlessness or privilege? I say, "Both and neither." Each time life travels around this circuit of change, it changes the very path it treads with its footsteps. Eating—the metabolic churning of matter—is like a lottery drum that constantly rearranges the variables of life. You are alive. You—a random, unique, and ever-changing constellation of matter—have won the ticket of *lila*. Time to play. Time to eat. Time to live.

An Eating Relay

Eating is metabolic give-and-take: just as you take, you give. This is the game of *lila* couched in thermodynamic and metabolic terms. In the words of biologist Lynn Margulis and science writer Dorion Sagan, "All organisms lead multiple lives. A bacterium attends to its own needs in the muds of a salt marsh, but it is also shaping the environment, altering the atmosphere. As community member it removes one neighbor's waste and generates another's food" (2001, 341).

Eating is the transmutation of energy and matter into energy and matter. Solar fire is converted into the green fire of photosynthesis, which is converted into the metabolic fire of cellular mechanics, which

is converted into the invisible fire of sentient aspirations, which is converted into the industrial fire of civilization building. All of us are
caught up in this Olympic-style relay of a life flame, passing it on from
a lung to a lung, from a mouth to a mouth, from a mind to a mind.
Appreciate your current role in this meal-wheel of living. What are you
going to do with this fire you swallowed, fire-eater? What will you
spark up, ignite, and set aflame with the energy you just consumed?
Will you share the sunlight you've digested? "Life is incessant heat-
dissipating chemistry," said Lynn Margulis and Dorion Sagan (2001,
341). What a heartwarming thought! So the next time you eat, ask
yourself, "Who am I passing this energy torch on to? How am I going to
dissipate this life heat? Who am I going to warm up with it?"

Share your mindful eating experiences online using the Mindful Eating
Tracker at http://www.eatingthemoment.com/mindfulness-tracker.

chapter 8

Reinventing Fasting

The Dao is present in emptiness. Emptiness is the fasting of the mind.

— Zhuangzi

Before we proceed, a caveat: If you have struggled with restrictive eating or have been diagnosed with anorexia, this chapter is not intended for you. You can read it, of course, but should you find it behaviorally compelling in any way, I suggest you find an experienced psychologist or psychotherapist to discuss this material and its relevance to you.

Eating—at its functional and existential core—is there to break a fast. Unlike plants, which generally have their food handed to them by the sun, animals have to work for a living. Animal life has to forage, hunt, or harvest (or shop, in our urban manifestation) before it gets to eat. Back in the evolutionary day, after a period of rest we'd awaken in a state of hunger and go gathering and hunting until we managed to procure some sustenance to break our hunger, to break our fast.

Eating only when necessary because we were hungry made sense for millions of years, and it still makes sense. The only time need-based eating didn't make sense was when food was unusually scarce. In that circumstance, overeating and feasting when possible made good survival sense. But agriculture changed everything. As a civilization we have ensured a reasonably steady supply of food, at least for most of us. Let's face it: if you're reading about mindful eating, chances are you aren't at risk for starvation, so overeating in preemption of hunger and using your body for mobile energy storage in case of a potential famine would be overkill.

This chapter is about reinventing fasting, about recognizing that *not* eating is also part of mindful eating. It isn't about prolonged cleansing fasts; it's about noticing and taking the daily opportunities for fasting that we mindlessly overlook as we get triggered to eat by the clock.

Time-Based Eating Is Mindless Overeating

Most of us have been culturally conditioned to eat at least three meals a day, typically a breakfast, lunch, and dinner. Thus, an eating day doesn't quite seem complete unless you've had all three of these, at a minimum. Our approach to eating is akin to a to-do list: gotta have breakfast, gotta have lunch, and gotta have dinner. And you gotta do it more or less at the culturally prescribed times: breakfasts are for morning, lunches are for midday, and dinners, or suppers, are to be saved until later in the day. This time-based three-meals-a-day paradigm overlooks the basic fact that our energy demands vary on a day-to-day basis and that no two days are the same. As a result, we eat when we don't feel like eating and don't eat when we do feel like eating—not because of the chaotic ebb and flow of the food supply, but because our eating follows a mind schedule rather than a body schedule. It's no wonder that this time-based eating results in mindless overeating. Allowing yourself to fast until you feel legitimately hungry is an opportunity to reunite body and mind in an act of conscious, mindful eating.

Every Meal Is a Break-Fast

The new meal paradigm views each meal as a break-fast, that is, as an intervention for mouth hunger, not for mind hunger. Perhaps this makes you nervous. Maybe you're subject to the commonplace fear that if you wait too long to eat and get too hungry, you'll be more likely to overeat. That concern isn't relevant here. I'm not suggesting that you wait until you're *too* hungry. I'm suggesting that you wait until you're just hungry enough to eat.

I recommend that you abandon the confusing meal language of "breakfast," "lunch," "brunch," "dinner," "supper," and "snack." I encourage you to instead retrain yourself to think of each meal as a break-fast. In this relabeling scheme, your first morning meal becomes "first break-fast." Whatever follows is the "second break-fast," whether by former terminology it would constitute a midmorning brunch, a midday lunch, or an early afternoon snack. Whatever follows that is "third break-fast," even if it happens to be what was formerly considered a dinner or supper.

If it's any consolation, the word "dinner" means "break-fast" anyway. It takes its origin from the Gallo-Romance verb *desjunare*, which meant "to break one's fast," originally from the Latin verb *disjejunare*, where *dis* means "undo," and *jejunus* means "fasting, hungry."

Letting go of your old-school meal language will help you cut the umbilical cord to time. In the new meal paradigm, the timing of a meal isn't about time per se; it's about your personal physiology and the timing of your actual hunger. You eat your first break-fast when you're ready to break your fast, not when it's time to have the morning meal. By semantically reframing each meal as a break-fast, you are liberating yourself from the arbitrary irrelevancies of time-based coordination. You will be pleased to discover that your eating will suddenly begin to be about you—as it should be!

Letting go of time-based meal designations also allows you to open up your nutritional options. There is absolutely no reason why your first break-fast has to involve cereal and toast. Our time-based meal notions come prepackaged with ideas about what is and isn't appropriate for a certain time of the day. This time-based way of structuring our menus is arbitrary cultural conditioning that has nothing to do with our present-moment preferences and nutritional demands and needs.

I realize that making this change will probably throw a major monkey wrench into the dynamics of your social life. I also realize that you might be a bit concerned about always having to wait until you're hungry to eat. Yes, it is a potentially stressful thought—unless, of course, you learn how to appreciate the meditative aspects of feeling hungry. But I get it. I don't like absolute rules either, and I'm not going to propose any absolutes myself. So let me clarify an important point: it's okay to eat when you aren't hungry. After all, you've been doing that for most of your life. So if you occasionally feel like having something to eat not because you're hungry but just because, then do it. It won't kill you. However, let's agree to call that eating experience what it is: not a meal, but a treat between your break-fasts.

Fast-Time Is Slow-Time

Having talked about break-fasts, now let's talk about the fasts themselves. There's nothing to fear about daily fasts. You already fast every day, on average for about eight hours, from the time you go to bed until you get up the following morning. Then you fast between your meals and snacks throughout the day. Fasting is simply not eating. But by reconceptualizing all your meals as break-fasts, you stand to slightly lengthen the fast-time between meals by making eating contingent on hunger rather than time. And by increasing the fast-time between your meals, you'll be actually adding some slow-time to your day-to-day living. Instead of scurrying to figure out what to eat for lunch, you might skip it because you don't feel hungry and spare yourself the midday hassle of a meal. Instead, you might decide to take that time to slow down and relax.

When we think of fasting, we typically envision long stretches of time without eating—days, maybe even weeks. That's not what daily fasting is about. Daily fasting is simply letting the downtime between meals extend, not through willpower and self-restriction, but naturally, because you are not yet ready to eat. Daily fasting is about letting the

· meal-wheel slow down by itself. It's also about consciously taking advantage of the downtime gained from not eating, using it for meditation, contemplation, and psychospiritual rejuvenation. Fasting is downtime for body and mind. And daily fasting means less time spent shopping and cooking too, and thus more life!

Health Benefits of Daily Fasts

According to calorie restriction and fasting experts, lengthening the fasting time between meals may help you extend your life span—and your health span. Calorie restriction is "an approach to health and longevity that contends that consuming fewer calories daily than your body is accustomed to will increase energy, and improve physical and cognitive health, and may add years to your life" (McGlothin and Averill 2008, xiii).

The approach I propose—daily fasting and relabeling meals as "break-fasts"—isn't intended as a calorie restriction program, though it might naturally become one. Writing as a psychologist, not as a nutritionist or physician, I'm discussing an approach to eating, not telling you how much to eat. I am merely drawing your attention to the basic fact that time-based eating is divorced from hunger and as such is a form of mindless overeating. However, if you semantically reframe all of your meals as break-fasts, you may well shift to hunger-based eating. This may naturally lengthen your fasting time and thereby naturally reduce overeating and unnecessary calories consumed. As such, this approach is compatible with the microfasting recommendations of the calorie restriction approach.

Calorie restriction research is based on the idea that "when our ancestors struggled through extended periods without food, the body's remarkable survival instinct would kick in and somehow slow down their aging" (McGlothin and Averill 2008, 3). Calorie restriction is an empirically driven eating program supported by breakthrough studies such as those by Clive McKay and Mary Crowell, who "showed that calorie restriction greatly extended the lives of mice" (McGlothin and Averill 2008, xiv). Calorie restriction isn't anorexia in disguise. The psychology behind anorexic eating is fundamentally different from that fueling the calorie restriction approach. Anorexia is about self-control through eating, whereas calorie restriction is about health and vitality.

Here's the rationale behind the calorie restriction regimen referred to as "daily limited fasting": "Time away from food [is] even more valuable than calorie restriction for increasing beneficial brain chemistry… The body responds to the stress of periodic fasting [by] triggering protective proteins in the brain and stimulating regeneration of brain cells" (McGlothin and Averill 2008, 82–83).

The calorie restriction model (just like the *oryoki* model) is a great example of skillfully reinventing the meal. It's a total bodymind attitude to eating. Those designing specific calorie restriction approaches have also explicitly incorporated the so-called "cephalic" (brain-based) factors of meditation into their approach. These cephalic factors are, in essence, mindfulness know-how. I encourage you to explore the calorie restriction literature when shopping for an eating lifestyle.

Trust the Hunger

In regard to daily fasting, my suggestion isn't based on the technicalities of glucose control and calorie intake. I invite you to begin from a far more intuitive place: a place of hunger. I encourage you to simply follow the lead of nature, and specifically your own nature, not of time, which is a mind-made construct. Basing your eating on time is like basing sex on time. We get physiologically turned on—to eat or to mate—when we get turned on, not when it's time to get turned on. Sure, our physiology can be conditioned to be aroused on cue, just like we can be conditioned to salivate at the chime of a bell. The mind is putty, utterly malleable and subject to conditional subjugation. However, I encourage you to break off this romance between your mind and time and rekindle the intimacy between your body and your mind through mindful eating *and* through mindful non-eating.

Developing Hunger Recognition Skills

By calling all meals break-fasts, you are reminding yourself of the physiological point of eating: to break a fast for the purposes of relieving hunger. To relieve hunger, you have to be able to recognize it.

Eating on the basis of hunger, not time, may sound foreboding to most eaters and undoubtedly will sound foreboding to most overeaters because of our cultural lack of familiarity with normal hunger. We fear what we don't know. Fret not: mindful daily fasting is fearless fasting. It's a calm and relaxed engagement with the ebb and flow of your metabolism, rather than a preemption of hunger with premature eating. The body knows what it needs. It's been in the business of sustaining itself since its first breath. If it's hungry and needs to eat, it will let you know. It will make itself heard—if you can hear it. The trick is to allow this to happen and not jump the gun by eating because of a craving or a schedule. Therefore, hunger recognition skills are part and parcel of mindful eating *and* mindful non-eating.

Learning to Differentiate Between Hunger and Cravings

Craving is a false hunger signal that mimics hunger. Cravings prompt us to eat as if we were hungry when we actually aren't. Hunger is a physiological need with a physiological signature, a body state. Craving, on the other hand, is a psychological state, essentially a thought of desire and therefore a state of mind. Hunger is generic: you need food—any food that will make hunger go away. Cravings are specific: you want a particular food. Hunger depends on your physiology. Cravings depend on the situational context. Hunger is triggered by an empty stomach. Cravings are triggered by food commercials. Successful mindful eating involves a clear understanding of these differences.

In his book *Fasting and Eating for Health*, Joel Fuhrman, MD, offers the following intriguing thoughts about hunger (1995, 18–19):

> True hunger is a mouth and throat sensation, felt in the same spot that one feels thirst. Gnawing in the stomach, stomach

cramping, headaches, and generalized weakness from not eating or skipping a meal or two are experienced only by those who have been eating the standard American diet with all its shortcomings (those most in need of a fast). Those who have been consuming a healthier, low-fat, low-protein, plant-based diet for months prior to the fast typically experience no such typical hunger pains when they fast. Symptoms such as abdominal cramping and headaches, traditionally thought of as hunger symptoms, are not really symptoms of hunger… These symptoms are signs of withdrawal that indicate healing is beginning when the body has the opportunity to rest from the continual intake of food.

I can certainly attest to this on the basis of my own experience. Having gone through a few water-only fasts, I can confidently say that you have nothing to fear from fasting, let alone from time-limited periodic fasting between meals. To help assuage your fear, try the following exercises. They'll help you get reacquainted with hunger.

Try This: Say Hello to Hunger

Chances are, you haven't had the experience of true hunger for quite some time, if ever. Sometime in the not-too-distant future, take the opportunity to feel genuine hunger. Not to worry: once you feel hunger, you can relieve it by eating. If you feel you should consult your physician about whether it's safe for you to delay a meal to experience a genuine state of hunger, by all means do so. Then, plan a day (preferably a day off) and abstain from eating until you get hungry. That's all there is to it. If you dare, push the envelope a bit and allow yourself to get very hungry. Note the physiological signature of this moment of hunger and say hello to its motivational urgency.

Try This: Contrast and Compare

Practice distinguishing between a state of hunger and a craving. In the days to come, when you feel like eating, reference your recent experience of genuine hunger (from the preceding exercise) and ask yourself, "Is the experience I'm having right now a state of hunger?" If the experience doesn't feel like hunger and seems to be a craving, ponder what triggered your craving. Note the duration of the craving. How long does it last? How quickly does it vanish? Shall you satisfy your craving? Just be sure to make it a conscious choice. Either way, ask yourself, "What have I learned about the difference between cravings and hunger?"

Try This: Observe a Micro Lent

The word "Lent" has its origins in an old English word for "spring," from the Anglo-Saxon verb meaning "to lengthen." While the Christian tradition of Lent is seasonal, I propose a daily celebration of the resurrection of your own body, a micro Lent, if you will. This is not a spiritual practice, and I'm not offering spiritual advice. My intent is merely to borrow a breath of inspiration from a culturally familiar and somewhat poetic tradition. The fact is, each and every day we all rise and awaken anew. The ancient Greek philosopher Heraclitus spoke to this with his aphorism "You can never step into the same river twice." This is also true for the river of body. Each and every one of us is a nonstop flow of existence, a metabolic current in the stream of life, renewing ourselves with each breath, with each bite, with each contact with reality.

The micro Lent that I propose is not a lengthening of the downtime between the meals, as when you make each meal a break-fast. This micro Lent is a contemplative lengthening of the breath in recognition of the metabolic churning of reality. More specifically, whenever you catch a glimpse of hunger, allow yourself to linger in that moment. Allow your breath to lengthen in awe of your dependence on reality. Here you are, once again reminded by your hunger of your fundamental interconnectedness with the river of existence. This urge to eat that you feel is the urge to connect. It is the urge to borrow some life force from the totality of what is. It is the urge to renew yourself.

So don't rush. Instead, let your breath lengthen. Celebrate this pending moment of nutritional resurrection. Or try the following thought (slightly paraphrased)—a reading recommended for Ash

Wednesday, the first day of Lent, by Unity Church founder Charles Fillmore: "I deny out of consciousness old error thoughts, as if I were gently sweeping away cobwebs, and I affirm positively and fearlessly that I am a child of [Reality]" (1999, 141). (Fillmore, of course, said "a child of God." I took the liberty of secularizing this thought.) So when you notice hunger in the days to come, clean out the cobwebs of thought with a long, sweeping out-breath and recognize, unafraid of hunger, that you are a child of Reality, and that Reality hasn't failed you yet. Affirm your connection with all that is during this fleeting moment of non-eating. Marvel at this transmigration of ash and dust: made of Earth, we are eating Earth, and Earth we become—positively and fearlessly.

Conclusion: The New Fast

The old fast was an ascetic undertaking extending over days, if not weeks. It was an austere blitz of dietary self-restriction. The daily fasting I propose here is different: it is simply mindful downtime between break-fasts and choosing to eat based on hunger. This approach is for anyone who's interested in cutting the umbilical cord to Father Time and reconnecting with Mother Nature. Mindful daily fasting isn't a deprivation; it's an opportunity for contemplative enrichment. Hardly anything is required of you. Simply rethink all of your meals from this point on as break-fasts and build your eating around the needs of your body rather than the habits of your mind. Mindful fasting is just the flip side of mindful eating.

An Amuse-Bouche of Pattern Interruption

Sometimes I hear people say that mindful eating is boring. Sometimes I counter with "Mindless eating is what's boring; that's why we tend to spice it up with the entertainment of TV." I'm not going to take that angle in this section. Instead, I simply invite you to enjoy the spice of pattern interruption. Entertain your mind before you open your mouth so that you don't have to rely on external entertainment while you eat. Mindful eating is its own reality TV.

Mouth on Fire

You might want to sit down for this one. You are on fire. In the metabolic sense, you are a slow flame, burning matter into the incandescence of awareness—literally. Ilya Prigogine, a chemist and Nobel laureate, thinks of life as a dissipative structure not unlike a flame. Indeed, a flame, just like life, "maintains itself (and may even grow) by importing [feeding itself] 'useful' forms of energy and exporting [excreting], or dissipating, less useful forms—notably, heat" (Margulis and Sagan 1995, 16). This thermodynamic view of life would not have surprised Allama Prabhu, a medieval poet of India, who wrote, "A burning fire is mouths all over" (Ramanujan 1973, 165). It's a metabolic axiom, both for the wood fire and the human candle: the faster you live, the faster you die. So mouth-on-fire, what's your rush? Can't wait to devour yourself? Consider slowing down your blaze of eating to a metabolically reasonable simmer. Leave the pilot light of mindful presence on. You are not a meth lab, you know.

A Grateful Living Grave

George Bernard Shaw wrote, "We are the living graves of murdered beasts slaughtered to satisfy our appetites." You see, food isn't just food; food is life. We—carnivores and vegans alike—don't eat food, we eat life. Lynn Margulis and Dorion Sagan expressed this well (1995, 30):

> The biological self incorporates not only food, water, and air—its physical requirements—but facts, experiences, and sense impressions, which may become memories. All living beings, not just animals but plants and microorganisms, perceive. To survive, an organic being must perceive—it must seek, or at least recognize, food and avoid environmental danger... Hundreds of millions of years before organic beings verbalized life, they recognized it. Discerning what could kill them, what they could eat, and what they could mate, roughly in that order, was crucial to animal survival... We all have a similar ability with life. Life has been recognizing itself long before any biology textbooks were written.

Mindful eating is about recognizing life as we eat. To fail to see life in food is to fail to say hello to our own origins, to our own predecessors. Mindful eating is a namaste greeting from one life-form to another: the life in me recognizes the life that this food once was. Whereas mindless eaters count disembodied calories and objectify cows into steaks, mindful eaters open their mouths (and their minds), first greeting the memory of the life they are about to consume before opening their mouths to consume it.

All life perceives as it pursues its own quota of well-being. All living bodies are living minds. Be mindful of the minds that animated the bodies you eat, be they plant or animal. Bid a farewell namaste as you bury their bodies in yours. Don't let your body become an anonymous graveyard of all the lives you've eaten. This journey isn't a guilt trip; it's an invitation to see all life as equal. Whether you have a steak for dinner every day or subsist solely on fruits that fall, ripe, from tree or vine, you are consuming life energy. Say hello to it and commemorate it with mindful presence as you eat.

The Eros of Eating

"Once upon a time, we think, eating and mating were the same," wrote Lynn Margulis and Dorion Sagan (1995, 139). Meiosis, the process of cell division that creates two offspring cells and is the foundation of reproduction, was originally "an urge not to merge but to eat" (139). "When protists of the same species devoured but did not digest each other, they sometimes merged nuclei and chromosomes, a commingling equivalent to the first act of fertilization or mating" (138). A cell would swallow a cell (out of hunger) and in so doing would end up exchanging genes. Sex, it seems, started out as a case of indigestion. Curious, huh? Eating and sex at some point were one and the same. To this day, both eating and sex are intimate exchanges of information. Both are events of unmistakable enmeshment, collisions of you and not-you, of the inner and the outer. First, there was life; then those early life-forms ran out of food and started eating each other, and sex was born. Ponder that the next time you wrap your mouth around a banana or lick yogurt out of a spoon. The orality of both food and sex speak to the secret of our origin. Relish the commonality of these activities. Yes, you are Earth that is eating itself. That's the Eros of eating. Enjoy it.

Noospheric Eating

According to Dorion Sagan, Russian-Soviet scientist Vladimir Vernadsky "pictured life on Earth as a global chemical reaction, a 'green burning' (1990, 39). He saw life—in all its mineral nudity—as "rock rearranging itself under the sun" (40). Vernadsky saw Earth as a living system and introduced the concept of "living matter," bridging the seventeenth-century Cartesian body-mind divide with one eloquent phrase of integration. He saw life in matter and matter in life. Pondering (according to Sagan), "What is a swarm of locusts from the biogeochemical point of view?" (46), Vernadsky proffered that it is "a disperse of rock, extremely active chemically, and found in motion" (46), or, as Sagan paraphrased, "an airborne stream of rock" (46). Along with

Pierre Teilhard de Chardin (sometimes dubbed the "evolutionary theologian"), Vernadsky popularized the terms "biosphere" (the sphere of *bios*, or sphere of life) and "noosphere" (the sphere of human intelligence), which Vernadsky saw as planetary layers (along with the geosphere, atmosphere, and stratosphere.

Keeping all of this in mind, there are two things to highlight. You've already heard me express the first one time and again: you are Earth eating Earth. Vernadsky probably would have agreed with this geochemical view of eating. Indeed, what is food but "bits of matter that have come detached from the Earth and are moving around" (Sagan 1990, 46)? And what are you, the eater, but "bits of matter that have come detached from the Earth and are moving around"? My second point is also Vernadskian in nature: When you eat mindlessly, you are nothing but biosphere, just a "rock rearranging itself under the sun." When you eat mindfully, you are part of the global noosphere, part of the sphere of conscious awareness—in essence, part of Earth's mind. So as your mouth moves around these "bits of matter that have come detached from the Earth," let your mind join the planetary noosphere of conscious consumption.

Share your mindful eating experiences online using the Mindful Eating Tracker at http://www.eatingthemoment.com/mindfulness-tracker.

chapter 9

Reconsidering the Ahimsa Meal

A man is not virtuous because he doesn't eat meat, nor is he any less virtuous because he does.

— Jiddu Krishnamurti, *Commentaries on Living*

Each one of us is a living grave of destruction and a dying womb of creation. We kill to eat, but in eating we also sustain an entire microcosm of invisible lives that inhabit our bodies and depend on us for existence. Indeed, each one of us is no less than a planet. Each human body is home to "a greater number of [microscopic] organisms...than there are people on earth" (Downer 1991, 171–179). According to William Logan in his book *Dirt: The Ecstatic Skin of the Earth*, "A full ten percent of our dry weight is not us, properly speaking, but the assembly of microbes that feed on, in, and with us" (1995, 55). Thus eating—perhaps more so than any other act of living—is a paradox of life taking and life giving and, as such, is a potential Gordian knot of ethics.

The practitioners of Jainism—an ancient Indian philosophy of living that predates Buddhism—understood the ethical intricacies of eating. Jains were the first to formulate the doctrine of ahimsa (a Sanskrit term for "nonviolence") and to apply it to eating. According to this doctrine, all souls, which Jains equate with consciousness, are the same, and "differences among souls are due to the degree of their connection to matter" (Radhakrishnan and Moore 1973, 250). It is from this position of equality of souls that the Jains called upon humans to be compassionate toward all life-forms.

This chapter is about reconsidering this noble ideal of "absolute noninjury" and understanding the essence of ahimsa rather than its vegetarian or vegan form. The problem with noble ideals is that they are fundamentally unattainable and tend to dehumanize what is human. Therefore, this chapter will explore conscious moderation, including moderation of compassion.

Extremes of Ahimsa, Extremes of Compassion

Mahatma Gandhi once wrote, "I must reduce myself to zero. So long as man does not of his own free will put himself last among his fellow creatures, there is no salvation for him. Ahimsa is the farthest limit of humility" (Gandhi 1999, 420). In my humble opinion, Gandhi is wrong on this point. First, we are not zeros, so why should we reduce ourselves to zeros? Ahimsa, as I understand it, is about equality of souls, not self-negation. Second, because we are not zeros (we exist, don't we?), we cannot reduce ourselves to zeros. Third, absolute nonviolence in the equation of existence is simply impossible. To live is to kill until the very last breath. Play with the following experiential meditations to appreciate what I mean.

Try This: Take a Bite of Zero-Sum

You are a microcosm of life, literally home to trillions of microscopic creatures. Even just your mouth is a micro metropolis in constant turmoil. In his book *Lifesense*, John Downer wrote that every time we eat, the bacterial population of the mouth "experiences a catastrophic collapse as [bacteria] are overwhelmed by torrents of food and saliva" (1991, 168). So go get a single bite of something and then eat it. As you annihilate countless microbes in your mouth, ponder the inevitability of this zero-sum arrangement. For the rest of your life—whether you are a vegetarian, vegan, or fruitarian, whether you're a locavore or an omnivore—each of your meals will be an act of bactericide. It's basic: you have to eat to live, but the mechanics of chewing wipe out an entire micropolis of living aspirations. You can shrug this off by exclaiming, "Are you kidding me?! It's just tiny, stupid little bacteria! Who cares?" But isn't this the very human arrogance that we rail against when we hear animal abusers rationalize their actions with that seventeenth-century Cartesian nonsense that animals are just biological automata that don't feel or suffer? Understand that there are no saints among living creatures: to live is to kill, no matter what you eat, because the very act of eating is inherently an act of violence, if only on a micro-scopic level. Ahimsa doesn't differentiate between souls and minds on the basis of their physical complexity. The point of ahimsa is that any-thing that is alive—no matter how small or large, no matter how complex or primitive—is worthy of compassionate consideration.

Try This: Wreak Havoc with a Swig of Mouthwash

A swig of mouthwash guarantees the death of legions of bacteria in your mouth. Any number of mouthwashes proclaim this widely and mince no words about killing germs that cause plaque, gum disease, and other unhealthful conditions. So there it is, the evolutionary battle for survival and the inevitable zero-sum of existence: if you don't kill these germs, they will cause you harm. It's either their well-being or your dental, cardiovascular, and relationship health. It's them or you. So take a swig of mouthwash and meditate on the inevitability of harm. I wonder if Gandhi would have objected to mouthwash. What do you think?

Try This: Save a Clove of Garlic, Kill a Clove of Garlic

A while back, while peeling a head of garlic I noticed that the cloves had begun to sprout. Tiny green shoots were poking out of their white husks. I broke off several cloves and stuck them into a pot of soil. A couple of days later, two-inch-tall green blades were proudly sticking out of the ground. Not having much of a green thumb, I was touched and amazed. "Garlic is also a life-form," I thought. "Each clove is alive, yearning for its moment under the sun and entirely at my mercy for its future." Make no mistake, there is no such thing as innocent eating. To experience this for yourself, get a head of garlic and rescue one clove by planting it, while killing another clove by cooking or eating it. Contemplate the inevitable arbitrariness of your choice: it is entirely up to you, human god, which garlic life-form gets to live and which must die. And remember, there is no need for guilt here. After all, if that clove of garlic could have eaten you instead to ensure its survival, it most certainly would have.

Zero Harm Is Impossible

Among his many notable political accomplishments, Gandhi was known for using fasting as a form of political protest. The idea of protest through fasting harkens back to the Jain tradition of *santhara*, a voluntary ritual of fasting until one's death. The vow of *santhara* is distinguished from suicide in that fasting until one's death is not an escape from distress but an open-ended end-of-life meditation and, in Jainism, a purging of negative karma. With all due respect to both Gandhi and the venerable tradition of Jainism, I see a glaring inconsistency between fasting and the principles of ahimsa. Recall that you are a living microcosm, a home to innumerable microscopic creatures—bacteria, fungi, parasites, and more, let alone your own cells. Indeed, each and every one of your cells has its own appetite, its own metabolism—and therefore its own existential agenda. All of this collective microbial and cellular existence depends on you. All of these innocent microscopic and cellular lives within your body will go down with you if you cut off your own supply of nourishment.

As I've said, life is a zero-sum game. We cannot avoid violence; we can only minimize it. The bottom line is that we actually cannot reduce ourselves to zeros even if we try. The very decision to reduce oneself to a metabolic zero (say, through starvation) instantly and unilaterally overrides the existential aspirations of legions of microscopic lives that depend on us for sustenance. Absolute nonviolence is a myth. Given that we are composite creatures, any decision to reduce oneself to zero—be it for spiritual, political, or psychological reasons—holds the rest of the bodily community hostage to one's idealism.

Thus, there's an inherent hypocrisy in justifying Gandhi-style self-reduction to zero on the grounds of ahimsa. Dorion Sagan and Lynn Margulis crystallize this well: "If we were truly serious about saving all other organisms, we would follow Jainist principles and…surgically implant chloroplasts in our skin in order to photosynthesize ourselves and not uproot lettuce or carrot plants. We certainly would not cavalierly flush away our solid wastes that serve as a breeding ground for *E. coli* and other gut bacteria. This reductio ad absurdum shows the hypocritical element implicit in the rhetoric of ecological salvation" (1993, 358). They're right: uprooting a carrot for human consumption is a form of violence, as is mindlessly flushing a toilet and decimating the bacterial colonies that make their home in our fecal matter. But like Gandhi, Sagan and Margulis are also off track. In its essence, ahimsa isn't really about avoiding all harm (which is technically impossible); it's about harm reduction.

Try This: Eat to Give Life

Eat a strawberry, and as you do so, contemplate this: By eating that strawberry you are denying its seeds a chance to sprout, flourish, and fully express their essence. And as you eat that strawberry, you are also annihilating innumerable bacteria that have made their home in your mouth since your last intake of food. And, most importantly, by eating that strawberry you are powering up innumerable invisible lives that reside within your body. Try to really appreciate this often-ignored piece of the eating puzzle: the very fact of eating gives life—not just to you (in your human understanding of yourself), but to all of your biological partners in the project of your body. Understand that this is true regardless of what you eat. Whether you are a strict vegan or an undiscriminating omnivore, whether you eat a carrot or a steak, each and every act of eating powers up a universe of invisible life. Meditate on this inevitable dialectic: to eat is to take life is to give life.

Ahimsa Eating Reconsidered

Ahimsa is not a do-no-harm philosophy. There is no such thing as a free lunch, or even a free breath. If you are living, you are consuming other life. If you are living, you are causing harm. Ahimsa is a harm-reduction philosophy that aims to minimize your ecological footprint to a compassionate minimum.

Jains reasoned that to eat is to take life, or kill, and therefore start a chain of karmic vendetta. In formulating their life stance, they drew an arbitrary line of division; they looked around and decided not to eat anything that looked like them or, more accurately, looked back at them. Jains basically decided not to eat what they could identify with, not to kill animals or insects for the purposes of eating them, and went vegetarian or vegan. They figured that since a stalk of rice doesn't yelp in pain as it's cut short or yanked out of the ground, it must not hurt, and therefore it must not be all that bad, karmically speaking, to consume it. This makes intuitive sense. Compassion is based on identification. If you can't identify with something, it's easier to perpetrate violence against it. If you can identify with something, if you can relate to it on some level, it's harder to mindlessly kill it. The bottom line is that Jains opted against eating creatures both out of compassion for creatures and in a self-serving attempt to minimize their own karmic or moral footprint.

Naturally, ahimsa-style eating has come to be synonymous with vegetarianism and veganism, and therefore with what you eat and don't eat. But what you eat and don't eat is ahimsa only in form, not in essence. In my understanding, the essence of ahimsa-style eating is about *how* you eat, not what you eat. If you eat mindlessly, you overconsume, no matter what you eat. If you overconsume, you overkill. Whether mindless eating kills more cows than necessary or mows down more wheat fields than necessary, it is still unnecessary overconsumption and thus unnecessary harm. Mindful eating, on the other hand, allows you to curb overconsumption and thereby reduce your zero-sum footprint to a functional minimum.

So my point is this: ahimsa eating is not about avoiding animal protein; it's about consciously reducing your metabolic footprint to a coexisting and compassionate minimum. You don't have to be a vegetarian or a vegan to eat in the spirit of ahimsa-style compassion; you just have to be mindful. Wherever there is mindfulness, there tends to also dwell compassion.

Honey-Eater Worse Than a Butcher?

According to Padmanabh S. Jaini, Professor Emeritus of Buddhism, Jainism, and Hinduism at the University of California at Berkeley, Jains are not necessarily strictly vegan. In fact, they would rather eat a steak than a spoonful of honey, as indicated by a verse from the *Yogasastra*, a twelfth-century text by Jain author Hemachandra: "One who eats honey, which is manufactured by the destruction of tens of thousands of tiny beings, is worse than a butcher, who only kills a single animal at a time" (as quoted in Moussaieff Masson 2009, 27).

But wait! Is the honey-eater really worse than a butcher? The Jain arithmetic seems a bit off here. If all souls are, according to ahimsa, equal, then isn't a single cow a far larger microcosm of microscopic lives and souls than an average beehive? It would seem so. But even if Hemachandra was mistaken in this soul calculus, ultimately that's not the point. The point is that ahimsa-style eating isn't a diet that dictates what you should and should not eat. Ahimsa-style eating is simply an attempt to reduce harm by eating with compassion and consideration for other lives, however insignificant they might seem. Ahimsa is prag-matic compassion, not righteous compassion.

To overeat is to overconsume, and therefore to trespass on life turf you really don't need to carve up and conquer, and therefore to engage in unnecessary violence. You don't have to be a vegetarian or a vegan to eat with compassion; you just have to be mindful. With this in mind, we can say that moderation is compassion. Moderation is the "how" of eating, not the "what" of eating. And it is this how—the how of modera-tion and mindful eating—that minimizes mindless overeating and thus minimizes unnecessary harm.

Compassionate Meat-Eating and Violent Veganism

Vegetarians and omnivores alike suffer from egocentric evangelizing. Each camp has its own antagonizing and proselytizing manifesto. This is a general human condition. We all like to promote our own values. But before doing so, we need to take at least a brief look in the mirror. None of us has a moral leg to stand on. All life is equal. That's one of the fundamental concepts of the ahimsa doctrine. By the same token, to kill is to kill. To take a life—whether of a person, a dog, a cow, a blade of grass, or a bacterium—is to play god. It's a sucky game, yet if we want to exist, we have to play it. But since we have to play this zero-sum game, let's try to enjoy it, responsibly and without guilt. There is no moral or ethical imperative (at least none that makes sense to me) requiring that we reduce ourselves to zero. Nor is it possible to entirely eliminate our metabolic footprint. As I see it, it is ethically sufficient to consciously reduce unnecessary harm to a compassionate minimum.

There is no moral pedestal, no eating without harm, no living without collateral damage. Even the strictest Jainist ascetics have to kill for a living. Wash your hands and you are committing bactericide. Bat your eyelashes and you are killing troops of tiny mites that have taken residence in them. Drive on a highway and your windshield becomes a battlefront. To live is to kill, and eating is no exception. To eat is to kill, regardless of what you are eating. We cannot avoid violence; we can only minimize it. Sure, we can ponder such questions as "Who takes more lives or causes more dietary destruction: a moderate meat eater or a vegan who overeats?" The finger-pointing mathematics of these kinds of inquiries seem irrelevant to me. What matters is that we attempt to redress the unnecessary harm of mindless overeating. And we can...by waking up.

Try This: Hug an Omnivore

If you are a vegan or vegetarian, find an omnivore you know and hug him or her or, if you aren't particularly touchy-feely, just shake hands. The point is to let go of any sense of ethical superiority over omnivores. There are no saints among us eaters. Whatever gesture you make, be sure you do it without condescension. And as you embrace the other or slide your hand into the other's hand, pay a mental tribute to all of the invisible lives that we erase with even this benign friction between our bodies. Unless you reside in a vacuum chamber, each step you take, each breath you breathe, each hand you shake, each mile you drive, and each bite you eat leaves an endless wake of microscopic destruction. So as you hug an omnivore, see a fellow eater—not an enemy, but an ally in this existence.

Try This: Become an "Om"nivore

Whether you are a meat eater, a vegetarian, or a vegan, put some om into your eating. Pay a moment of tribute to the life you consume. There's no need to feel guilty. Guilt and compassion are as different from one another as stiletto heels and refrigerators are. Simply devote a moment of thought to recognition, perhaps "This isn't just food; this used to be alive" or, as in the case of the sprouting garlic and other similarly "live" foods, "This is still alive. I am not just eating food; I am consuming life." Try this out and see what changes. Try thinking of yourself not just in terms of *what* you eat, but in terms of *who* you eat. Move beyond the savoring type of mindfulness to mindfulness of the life that you consume. Say a namaste to the potato in your bowl. Let the life in you recognize the life in the food that you eat.

Ahimsa Eating Restated

Old-school ahimsa eating is essentially synonymous with compassion-ate eating, veganism, and vegetarianism. New-school ahimsa eating—as I dare to posit—means eating consciously, compassionately, and in moderation, regardless of your choice of food. Mindless overeating exacts unnecessary harm, whereas mindfully eating in moderation reduces unnecessary harm. Understood as such, ahimsa-style eating doesn't necessarily equate with vegetarianism or veganism.

Conclusion: Heterotroph's Dilemma

There are those who produce energy and those who consume it. Plants are energy producers. They are known as *auto*trophs because they are nutritionally autonomous, requiring only sunlight, air, water, and min-erals. Self-feeding, they don't have to kill for living (with the rare excep-tion of carnivorous plants, such as the Venus flytrap). And then there are the rest of us. Animals of any kind—mammals, birds, insects, fish, and we humans—consume others; we are *hetero*trophs (*hetero* meaning "other"). That's our existential hell: to live we have to kill, and there's no way around it (at least not yet).

This dynamic is too natural to be an issue of ethics. Nature is beyond ethics. Ultimately, I see heterotrophic eating not as a matter of ethics, but as an existential predicament: we are trapped in a death-propagating cycle. But—and this is going to sound like science fic-tion—we don't have to stay on this circuit of existential hell. We can evolve. In our dim, distant origins, we share a lineage with plant life. This opens the door to the possibility that we can, at least in theory, also learn to produce energy. We can learn (or relearn) how to photosynthe-size. I'll come back to this in a later chapter. In the meantime, I leave you with a call for ahimsa—not with a call for nonharm or nonviolence (at this point, that's possible only for plants, not for animals), but with a call for harm reduction. Kill only as much as you need, and do it with compassion and gratitude, whether you are of the meat-eating or plant-eating persuasion. Let me close this chapter as I began. with the words of Jiddu Krishnamurti, "A person is not virtuous because he doesn't eat meat, nor is he any less virtuous because he does" (1977, 166). A person is virtuous because he or she is conscious of others. And wherever there is consciousness of others, there tends to dwell compassion.

An Amuse-Bouche of Pattern Interruption

In chess, a mind makes a dozen moves while the body sits motionless. It's the same with the game of mindful eating: move your mind before you turn on the ignition key of a hand-to-mouth trance. Change the game opener to change the endgame of eating. Open your meal with a moment of contemplative pattern interruption.

Hurricane Mouth

In the words of physicist Fritjof Capra, "A living system [in other words, you] is both open and closed—it is structurally open, but organizationally closed. Matter continuously flows through it, but the system maintains a stable form...through self-organization" (1997, 169). This is akin to Ilya Prigogine's concept of dissipative structures. As a living system, you take in matter from the environment and dissipate, or disperse, it back out in the service of self-maintenance. You do so primarily through eating. "Dissipation" is actually a bit too tactful a name for this process. You import order and structure, and you export disorder (in comes a life-form, such as a chicken or a carrot, and out goes waste). Eating destroys the structures of other living systems in order to maintain the structure of the destroyer. This self-serving metamorphosis of order into disorder is the essential process of life. Life maintains its own structure by deconstructing the environment it lives in. This is the Shiva paradox of eating: life destroys life to create life.

In a sense, you are just like the vortex of a hurricane, as Capra points out: "The dissipative structures formed by whirlpools or hurricanes can maintain their stability only as long as there is a steady flow of matter from the environment through the structure. Similarly, a living dissipative structure, such as an organism, needs a continual flow of air, water, and food from the environment through the system in order to stay alive" (1997, 172). So there you have it: your mouth is the funnel of a metabolic hurricane. Before you turn another buffet into a swath of destruction, mentally retrace your dissipative steps. If only for a moment, ponder the mountains of living and mineral structures you've moved—*with* your mouth, *into* you, *through* you, and *out* of you. Marvel at the sheer amount of energy it took to extract the energy you need to keep you on your rampage of catabolism (energy consumption). You are a mobile power plant unto yourself—a sentient hurricane! An old Zen koan comes to mind: Does a dog have Buddha-nature? In other words, can a dog awaken and become enlightened? Can a hurricane? Can you?

Ballistics of Eating

Plants are anabolic (energy producing) during the day and catabolic (energy consuming) at night. Animals are catabolic full-time. Unlike plants, animals don't produce energy; we just consume it. The word "catabolism," which means "destructive metabolism," comes from Greek word *katabole*, meaning "throwing down," having its roots, in turn, in *kata* (down) and *ballein* (to throw). When you consider that the English word "ballistics" refers to the art, science, and sport of throwing things, you can see that catabolism is the modern-day sport of eating. We play mindless metabolic football and then repeat our overeating mistakes ad nauseam, often through instant replay. Culturally, we turn any pretext for celebrating into a Super Bowl party of catabolism, with our gullets as the ultimate end zone.

It's time to consider a new national sport, a sport of mindfulness, witnessing, contentedness, and presence. You know that party trick people do where they toss up a nut or a piece of popcorn and catch it in their mouth? Well, that's not what your mouth is for. It's not a catcher's mitt. Your mouth is more like the eye of a needle; you need to carefully thread a lifeline of sustenance through it. Before your next meal, take a minute to bask in the moment. Feel the psychoanabolism of mindfulness. Note the life energy already available simply in the air that courses through your lungs. Take a deep breath and set a precedent of energizing yourself without having to throw anything down your throat.

Eater Yesterday, Food Tomorrow

The Celtic classic *Book of Taliesin* includes a poem purportedly by the sixth-century bard Taliesin, telling the story of his past lives (quoted in Wood 2000, 86–87):

> The second time I was created, I was a blue salmon. I was a dog, I was a stag; I was a roe-buck on the mountain side, I was a treasure chest, I was a spade; I was a hand-held drinking horn; I was a pair of fire-tongs for a year and a day; I was a speckled white cock among the hens of Eiden, I was a stallion standing at stud; I was a fierce bull; I was grain growing on the hillside... The hen, my enemy, red-clawed and crested, swallowed me. For nine nights I was a little creature in her womb; I was ripened there. I was beer before I was a prince. I was dead, I was alive.

In a way, isn't this the story of all of our yesterdays and tomorrows? Yesterday you were an eater of food. Today—if it all works out—you will hopefully still be an eater of food. But one of these tomorrows, you will be food yourself. Ponder your journey, living matter.

From Eating Glass to Eating Mirrors

Londoner and stuntman Terry Cole holds over 150 Guinness World Records. He also eats glass. "Well," he told a journalist in an interview, "I eat light bulbs. It's... I mean, I eat glass, not on a regular basis at all. But if the work comes in, then I'll do it" (Lawrie 1998, 243). Well then, I'm relieved. I'm glad that Terry eats glass not every day, but only when the work comes in. Eating glass—and eating in general—is work. Not as much for the jaws (Terry pregrinds the glass) or for the stomach (which in Terry's case must be made of iron), but for the mind. I dig people like Terry—not because they eat glass, but because it takes a lot of mind to pull off something like that. Mindful eating is sort of the same: it's like eating mirrors. Mindful eating is reflective eating that shows you *you*. So have a mirror sandwich for breakfast.

Creative Destruction of Eating

In the words of Lynn Margulis and Dorion Sagan, "Photosynthesis has stored solar energy in rocks as reserves of kerogen, oil, gas, iron, sulfide, coal, and other substances. The planet's prodigal species [*Homo sapiens*, that is] now expends these reserves… Our creative destruction accelerates" (1995, 242). Like the Indian god-concept of Shiva, the source of creative destruction, we turn the planet into a milkshake of processed landscapes and foodstuffs. Sure, you can busy yourself pondering such questions as "How many calories are in this?" Or you can ask yourself a different kind of question, a question of accountability, such as "How sustainable is my eating? Is my eating a regenerative form of sustenance or a net drain on the planetary expense sheet? What am I creating with this creative destruction of eating? In eating Earth, what kind of Earth am I becoming—an Earth of mindlessness or mindfulness, an Earth of presence or just another geological layer?"

Open Wide

Nature is perhaps the ultimate wheel. In *The Celtic Book of Living and Dying*, Juliette Wood wrote, "Nature both gives and takes life, and these two opposite aspects are completely interdependent: nothing can flourish or be healed without destruction" (2000, 26). Eating is destruction (of plant and animal bodies). Eating is also construction (of plant and animal bodies). Add the former to the latter and try to swallow the following contradiction without choking up on dualistic logic: destruction is construction. Open your mind far wider than your mouth to accommodate the paradox of eating.

Share your mindful eating experiences online using the Mindful Eating Tracker at http://www.eatingthemoment.com/mindfulness-tracker.

chapter 10

Reconciling Social Eating and Mindful Eating

To truly listen to another is a main course of the family's inner meal.

— Donald Altman, *Art of the Inner Meal*

Mindful eating is a rather personal endeavor. It's about self-synchronization. As such, mindful eating is best served solo. Yet we are social creatures. We like to connect with each other, particularly through eating. This chapter is about reconciling mindful eating with social eating, commingling them into mindful social eating.

Social Eating Is Time-Based, Not Hunger-Based

While several humans can, more or less, coordinate their minds into one meeting or one conversation in one moment, we often can't coordinate the physiology of our metabolic readiness. We can't sync up our stomachs. Therefore, the major problem of social eating is that it requires eating when you aren't ready to eat or getting too hungry because you've been waiting on others to get hungry enough. Either scenario heightens the chance of overeating. Because social eating involves time-based coordination, it is inevitably and inescapably time-based eating, not hunger-based eating.

Social Eating Is a Groupthink Process

The challenges of social eating aren't limited to its time-based commencement. Any gathering of eaters basically acts like spokes of one and the same wheel of appetite. This group eating-wheel starts rolling together as one and stops rolling together as one. I order an appetizer; you order an appetizer. You have a dessert; I have a dessert. People who eat together overeat together. Social eating is a kind of eating groupthink: a social attunement at the cost of losing touch with yourself. This kind of entraining, or unconscious coordination of activity, is part of human nature. We are pack animals. We take cues from each other. We have mirror neurons that turn on this "monkey see, monkey eat" behavior. You yawn; I yawn. I reach for a cookie; you reach for a cookie. This is neither good nor bad. It's just another potential overeating cue to watch.

Social Eating Is Distracting

Unless it is an *oryoki* group ceremony, a typical social eating event is primarily a get-together and only secondarily a meal. When we share the table, food tends to take the backseat to talk. I'll be blunt: companions are a distraction from eating. The larger the group, the harder it is to stay focused on the meal. Therefore social eating is almost always mindless eating. The mind is simply too divided to devote attention to food.

Yet mindless eating tends to be unsatisfying, particularly if you've gone out to eat somewhere special. As you fill up on the social calories of the moment, at some level the mind still craves a quality eating experience. So when the talk dries up or the main course comes to an end, it's not unusual to feel psychologically dissatisfied even if you feel physiologically and socially stuffed. The old-school remedy is all too simple to be effective: order dessert. Although dessert briefly awakens the group mind by refocusing it on taste, this doesn't last. Typically, the sensory experience quickly fades into the background and the dessert is finished off on autopilot. In sum, socialization is distraction and distraction is the nemesis of attention, which is, of course, required for mindful eating.

Social Eating Is Emotional Eating

Just because people voluntarily sit down to eat together doesn't mean they're going to enjoy each others' company. It's not unusual for the conversation to deteriorate or even become flat-out hostile. Because you have food in front of you, it's natural to cope by eating. This tends to happen mindlessly. Before you know it, you pull back and barricade yourself behind food.

Social eating doesn't even have to turn ugly to lead to emotional eating. The conversation might be actually highly enjoyable and stimulating. Yet this good stress can also trigger emotional eating. Maybe you're getting too excited, so you begin to soothe yourself with food. Or maybe you're eager to speak and tired of someone monopolizing the conversation, so you passively aggress against the food on your plate. Or maybe, as is often the case, you are neither stressed nor excited but just bored with the conversation. Trapped at the table, you find stimulation in food. Regardless of the emotional flavor of the gathering, the social context emotionalizes the mind. And an emotionally hijacked mind with food in front of it is a ticking bomb of overeating.

From Mindless Social Eating to Mindful Social Eating

So, social eating is time-based (not hunger-based), distracting, a potential trigger for emotional eating, and often under the sway of groupthink. And yet it is the cultural ideal of a good time and family time. What can we do? We have to shift the paradigm from mindless social eating to harm reduction through mindfulness-based social eating. Here are a few ideas you might try for shifting the attention and intention of eating in social contexts.

Try This: Shift Focus from a Feast to a Fiesta

Cultures all around the world celebrate with food. Festivities have become synonymous with feasts. Here's a new meal attitude to try: have a fiesta without having a feast. The word "fiesta" originates from the word *festus*, which is Latin for "joyous." The essence of a holiday is celebration, and eating is but one way to rejoice. Experiment with celebrating a single holiday in a way that isn't food-centered—in a manner that is joyous but not gluttonous. Start simple. If a particular heavy-eating event has been a long-standing tradition (say, Thanksgiving), leave it alone—at least for now. Try out this fiesta-not-feast mentality on a more personal occasion when you have the prerogative to choose the format of the celebration. Enjoy enjoying with or without food. For example, instead of going out to a restaurant to celebrate your birthday, enjoy a picnic. In addition to eating, commune with nature and maybe throw a Frisbee. This way you'll have a celebration that involves some eating without being primarily focused on food.

Try This: Shift Focus from Social Eating to Social Savoring

Socialize to savor. Make food a talking point. Show curiosity about others' eating experience and model interest in the food in front of you. If you're eating different foods, offer others a taste of what you're having and ask others what they think. Assume the role of a mindful eating cheerleader: tactfully but persistently keep refocusing the conversation back on the food. Agree to indulge in quality, not in quantity. Go to some place exotic and eat something new. Save the shoptalk and the drama for later.

Try This: Shift Focus from "All You Can Eat" to "All You Can Taste"

The human tongue is a thrill seeker. As it tires of one taste, it looks for another. This sensation-seeking tendency of the tongue is what accounts for the phenomenon of sensory-specific satiety. Recall what happens at a buffet: while you might feel too full to eat another plate of roast beef and mashed potatoes, you wouldn't mind trying something else. When coupled with the distraction of social eating, sensory-specific satiety is a liability that can lead to overeating. So leave room for the curiosity of your tongue. Adopt a new attitude toward buffets, potlucks, and other kinds of smorgasbords. See them as gustatory galleries and peruse, don't abuse. Shift from an "all you can eat" mentality to "all you can mindfully taste" mentality. Invite your companions to join you in this approach.

Try This: Shift Focus from a Mouthful of Food to a Mouthful of Words

Social eating is a compromise from the get-go. You need to manage your expectations. Accept that social eating is mostly a harm-reduction project. Keep your mind awake even if you're in the company of eating zombies. Sneak in a few deep breaths to relax any stress you're bringing to the social table. Remember to open your mind before you open your mouth. Preload on air and water. Prime your mind to watch for those stomach-distention cues. Use your choice-awareness and pattern-interruption tricks to stay awake throughout the meal. Order something exotic or unfamiliar to tickle the curiosity of your mind. Don't worry about outing yourself as a mindful eater; part of mindful social eating is being willing to model and share your mindful eating know-how. Also give yourself permission to stand out; it's okay if everyone else is eating and you aren't. You have the existential right to feel full. So kick around the conversation ball and keep it in the air for a while. Ironically, a mouthful of words is an excellent defense against mindless eating.

Try This: Shift Focus from a Mouthful of Food to an Earful of Attention

As you may recall from the beginning of this chapter, Donald Altman, a psychotherapist and former Buddhist monk, said, "To truly listen to another is a main course of the family's inner meal" (1999, 101). His point is well-taken. After all, social eating isn't just about nutritional calories; it's about social calories as well. Being there for each other is also a form of nourishment. While it might seem that having your mouth full of food is a convenient way to bide time while someone else is talking at the table, allow yourself to simply sit sometimes, neither chewing nor talking but just listening. Remember: an empty mouth is an earful of attention.

Conclusion: From Collective Appetite to Collective Mindfulness

For some families, couples, and groups of friends, eating is a relational crutch and appetite is just about the only feeling they share with each other. In such cases, collective appetite is nothing more than collective mindlessness. But it need not be this way. If you like connecting with others through eating, do so mindfully. Put mindfulness back on the collective menu. Eating is a powerful common denominator. Take it a step further and turbocharge social eating occasions with mindfulness. Breaking bread mindfully will deepen your social connections.

An Amuse-Bouche of Pattern Interruption

Patterns put the mind to sleep. Pattern breaks wake the mind up. Any awakening is, fundamentally, a meditation on the difference between illusion and reality, an opportunity to see yourself anew. So have another course of pattern interruption to meditate on who is eating.

The Root of the (Living) Matter

In the next several meditations, I use Shiva-inspired poetry as a launching pad for pattern-interruption provocations in regard to eating. When I speak of such Hindu concepts as *lila* (the divine play, or cosmic drama) or Shiva (the agent of creative destruction), I neither profess nor promote dogma, I'm just playing the *lila* of words, using ideas to destroy a clichéd view of eating in order to create a new vision of eating. As I see it, the idea of Shiva is a particularly useful meme and a potent dialectic principle that helps explain the metabolic mystery of life. To explore these concepts, I'll be sharing a few lines from the Shiva-inspired poets Basavanna, Mahadevi, and Dasimayya, who seem to have had a great grasp of this creation-destruction tango of the cosmos.

Basavanna, a twelfth-century saint-poet, wrote, "The root is the mouth of the tree: pour water there at the bottom and, look, it sprouts green at the top" (Ramanujan 1973, 80). Animals—humans included—are akin to mobile plant life, with our root on top, where the mouth is. Pour in water up there, stuff that mouth up there with food, and, look, body sprouts below. Just like trees, we are living input-output tubes, just oriented differently and spatially liberated by our legs. Mouth is the root, the source, the starting point of all of your bodymind growth. You literally sprout from the very lips that kiss reality with every bite, from the two rows of teeth that mill the matter of reality into the consciousness that reads this sentence. So when you next sit down to eat, first notice your mouth. Clench and relax your jaws, chop your matter-milling teeth, smack your lips, and let your tongue maniacally sweep around its cavernous abode. Check the equipment that allows for your growth. Get rooted in your mouth. And realize that this reality you are about to process is the very ground you sprout from.

A Mouthful of Reflection

Consider this verse by Basavanna: "The eating bowl is not one bronze and the looking glass another. Bowl and mirror are one metal. Giving back light one becomes a mirror" (Ramanujan 1973, 90). Although we generally don't make bowls and mirrors out of bronze these days, a bowl is still a mirror. Mindfulness is the light inside your skull, a source of inner illumination. Next time you eat, notice the reflection of your face in the polished concave of the spoon you just emptied. Have a spoonful of reflection, eater. Enlighten and be enlightened by your own presence. Here you are, a mirror unto yourself. Next time you drink a sip of something, notice the reflection of your face in the surface of the liquid mirror. Here's *you* looking at you, kid! Recognize that eating is an opportunity for self-reflection.

A Plateful of Humility

"My body is dirt, my spirit is space," wrote Akka Mahadevi, a twelfth-century female devotee of Shiva (Ramanujan 1973, 116). This applies to all of us. Yes, your body is dirt—not in the sense of being unclean or undeserving, but simply being soil. You eat soil, then you soil yourself, and then you become soil. The words "human" and "humility" both derive their meaning from the word "soil." Recognize that you are simply a dish of ground-up Earth, served hot. As you eat, feel the humility inherent in the process and of your being. Ponder the bigger picture of all this as you are renewed, from the ground up, with each bite. Eating humbles us all. But there's no need to eat humble pie. Just have a serving of humility.

Body Is a Temple, Food Is the Sacrament

Indian architecture offers an intriguing reversal of the concept that the body is a temple, as described by Indian poet and scholar A. K. Ramanujan (1973, 20):

> Indian temples are traditionally built in the image of the human body. The ritual for building a temple begins with…planting a pot of seed. The temple is said to rise from the implanted seed, like a human. The different parts of a temple are named after body parts. The two sides are called the hands or wings, the *hasta*; a pillar is called a foot, *pada*. The top of the temple is the head, the *sikhara*. The shrine, the innermost and the darkest sanctum of the temple, is a *garbhagrha*, the womb-house. The temple thus carries out in brick and stone the primordial blueprint of the human body.

Nifty—but entirely unnecessary. Here's what Basavanna had to say on the topic: "The rich will make temples for Siva. What shall I, a poor man, do? My legs are pillars, the body the shrine, the head a cupola of gold. Listen, O lord of the meeting rivers, things standing shall fall, but the moving ever shall stay" (Ramanujan 1973, 20).

Indeed, why imitate what you already have? Your body is a temple. Why build another one? For that matter, why burn the gas to drive yourself to where you are not in the name of worship? Why not worship at home? What do I mean by "worship"? I mean love. However you want to see the ultimate source—Reality, Creation, Universe, Dao, Cosmos—find a way to connect to it, from within and without brokers. Even if your body isn't a temple, it certainly has one. Touch your index finger to the side of your head to point to the cupola of golden presence inside the brick-and-mortar of your skull. And as you next partake of the sacrifice of life that is food, sanctify it with your presence. When you know yourself, there is no need to go any farther than where you are. You have built (and are building) this temple of a body; now populate it with presence.

Nonpredatory Touch

Eating is predatory touch—touch turned into destruction. The first touch is taste, as the molecules of flavor intermingle with the tongue. Then we must grind the food down to a pulp (touching it again and again) before we swallow it. Then we digest (and therefore again touch) the food through chemical hand-to-hand combat. We certainly touch the food as it moves through us, along the length of the digestive tract—the tube that runs through us—in a kind of gustatory massage of peristalsis wherein we are now touched by the reality we swallowed. Mahadevi suggested another option: "Finger may squeeze the fig to feel it, yet not choose to eat it" (Ramanujan 1973, 133). Indeed, why not, every now and then, touch food without eating it? Why not, on occasion, take the predatory element of touch out of eating? Rescue one of the apples you brought home from its digestive fate by tossing it out the window. Let the random chaos of nature do the chewing for you this time. Set a precedent of nonpredatory, nonutilitarian touch. For a change, let food be something other than food, and let yourself be more than just an eater.

Fire of Hunger

Dasimayya, a tenth-century Shiva-inspired poet, wrote, "In the plate of food eaten after much waiting—a fire" (Ramanujan 1973, 99). Yes, hunger is a fire, a burning, an urge, a mobilizing force. Kindle it now and then. Let the flames of desire build up. Let the spark of your dependence on reality grow. Sit—in a moment of contemplation—in front of a plate of food. Let a mindful wait fan the flames of hunger and whet your appetite. Watch the fire of interest grow. People tend to think that mindful eating is boring. I say it's just the opposite: mindless eating is boring, which is why we keep spicing it up with TV, Internet, and reading. Hunger-primed mindful eating is about as boring as being on fire and then satisfying that ripened need with intense relief. When satisfied prematurely, hunger fizzes out like a match in the rain.

Think of it this way: The word "ravenous" is related to the word "robbery," and a ravenous appetite is clearly a violent, rash appetite. The word "ravenous" is rooted in "ravine," a gully hollowed out by a rapid and often violent flow of water. In Middle English, the word "ravine" meant "booty," "robbery," or "plunder." This is also connected to the verb "ravish" and the adjective "ravishing." Well-timed and well-developed hunger satisfies itself with force; it seizes the reality on which it feeds. It's a true Shiva moment of creative destruction. Therefore, mindful eating doesn't have to mean eating slowly. It can be rapid or intense. Mindfulness has nothing to do with speed—with fast or slow; it has to do with living at the speed of life. Mindfulness isn't a boring drag; it's an all-out engagement with reality. It isn't a dropping out; it's a plugging in. When you're bored, engage in a bit of foreplay with this fire of hunger. Let the flames of appetite shoot up. Let the yielding of the food douse it. Have a Shiva moment of destruction and renewal.

Share your mindful eating experiences online using the Mindful Eating Tracker at http://www.eatingthemoment.com/mindfulness-tracker.

chapter 11

Rethinking Obesity

I am, indeed, a king because I know how to rule myself.

— Pietro Aretino

This chapter is a conceptual provocation, an attempt to jolt your mind into a new understanding of obesity—not as weight gain but as loss of self. This (subjective) phenomenological view of obesity is tricky but motivationally valuable. So bear with me for a few pages.

You Are Not Your Body

You are not your body. I mean this literally, not metaphorically. Take your skeleton, for example. While you certainly need this collection of bones and joints, you are not this collection of bones and joints. How can that be? Because you don't really depend on any one of these skeletal parts to be the psychological or subjective you that you are. As a case in point, modern-day surgical medicine routinely replaces a variety of joints with cadaver parts or synthetic versions. And yet those who undergo these surgeries remain existentially the same. This is also true of our organs. With the help of modern-day transplant medicine, we can thrive by taking advantage of someone else's kidney or liver or heart. So we obviously aren't our organs. It goes without saying that we are not our body fluids. We drink, we urinate, and yet we remain the same. Likewise, we can donate blood without any psychological loss of self and receive transfusions of someone else's blood without becoming that someone else. Nor are we our tendons and muscle fibers, or our limbs. We can lose a limb or two, or even four, and still continue to be our psychological, subjective selves, particularly with the help of the latest Borg-like prosthetic technology that can be surgically wired right into the nervous system. And the same goes for our adipose tissue, or fat. Obviously we are not this tissue, otherwise we couldn't survive a liposuction without a loss of self. So then what are we?

The answer would seem to be the brain, right? But what is the brain? It isn't just the sum total of the billions of neurons inside your skull; it also includes the bodywide network of neural wiring. The brain is everywhere your nerves are. Perhaps you've never really thought of it this way, but the nerves that run throughout your body aren't just independent neural wiring. They are actually branches of the neurons that reside in your skull and spinal column. Thus, the brain is a neural network distributed all over your body.

You Are a Neural Tribe

To clarify, you are not just the brain in your skull; you are your entire nervous system. All of this neural wiring is you. To get what I mean, look at your hand. Now touch your palms together. The sensation of touch in your hands is conducted by the sensory nerves that are part of this neural network that you are. You are everywhere your nerves are, and you are in more than one place at a time: you are both in your left hand and in your right hand at the very same time—and in your skull as you ponder your neural omnipresence.

Okay, that was probably a bit trippy. But that's not the point. The point is that in a manner of speaking you aren't the brain either. The brain is the outside of what you are. You are actually inside of the brain, the mind-side of the brain, if you will. You are the subjective experience of your neural network—the flow of information within you. Mind is what this distributed nervous system feels like. You are the sum-total here-and-now feeling of this neural tribe of neurons and neural wiring.

And here's the kicker: this neural "you" lives inside this body that is not you. That's right, you—the mind you—exist within the medium of your body. Your body—with all of its bones, joints, fluids, organs, limbs, and adipose lining—is just the environment you live in.

Now if you want to get technical and anatomical, we can say that you are the mind-side (the subjective feel) of your nervous system, which itself is a combination of the central nervous system (your brain and spinal cord) and the peripheral nervous system (the neural wiring that extends throughout your body). So let's take a look at this neural wiring for a moment. What's it for? It's there to control various aspects of your body. Restated, this neural wiring is there to control your bodily habitat. Consequently, we can say that you are what you are (brain plus neural wiring), along with whatever it is that you can consciously and voluntarily control. Put differently, you are a domain of self-presence and a domain of control.

You (the mind-side of this distributed neural network) live inside a bodily perimeter, coexisting with other living components (your organs, muscles, fat cells, and so on), which are attached to a structure (your skeleton) and serviced by a living plumbing system that transports body fluids. So consider yourself to be a tribe of neural cells that governs the mobile dominion of a body that itself is comprised of various cellular tribes attached to the mineral chassis of a skeleton. You are a stand-alone cellular species (neurons) inside a cellular collective of fellow bodily species, a neural tribe amidst a body nation.

Let me clarify what I mean by a neural tribe: Your brain isn't really one continuous organ per se, but a community of neural cells (neurons) in collaborative communication with each other. Each of these neurons stands alone, separated from the rest of the network by synaptic gaps. Thus each neuron is its own mini life-form inside the neural tribe that you are. On a cellular level you are not one; you are many. You are a composite, a flock of consciousness, a neural beehive of activity distributed over the cellular real estate of your body, which in turn is not one continuous body per se, but a giant, mobile multicellular colony. You are a neural complexity within a larger environment of bodily complexity. You are a neural tribe within a larger bodily nation. And you are also the monarch of this sovereign body-land—at least in theory.

Think of this "you"—this distributed neural network that is reading this puzzling perspective—as a kind of neural driver inside the vehicle of your body. This body that you live in is like an RV (recreational vehicle) that you can park overnight to rest in or take out on the road of life in search of experience, sustenance, and perhaps even well-being. Sounds like an adventure! But there are a few problems: This vehicle might sometimes need maintenance. You—the neural driver of this bodily RV—might fall asleep at the wheel, or you might lose your capacity to steer. But let's put these metaphors aside and approach the question head-on: How does obesity threaten your sense of self and your sense of control over this bodily habitat?

Loss of Control, Loss of Self

Some of this body, this cellular matter around you, is within your control, but some of it isn't. For example, many of your muscle tissues are innervated by your conscious volitions. You can neurally manipulate, or control, these muscles. To see what I mean, squeeze a fist. Without you—your choice, your intention, your neural command—this hand is just there, living its own cellular life but ever ready to serve you, the neural tribe.

While muscle tissues are metabolically and existentially on their own, you—the mind—are strategically represented at all the critical outposts where your muscles are activated with the help of nerve endings. So muscles work for you. They are your proxies, your surrogates, your vassals. While anatomically separate from you, the muscle tribe is functionally you—as long as it behaves and obeys your neural commands.

What about adipose tissue, or fat? The fat tribe is inert. It is not innervated. Try to wiggle a spot of cellulite through intention alone, without manipulating it, to see what I mean. You can move your thigh, but you can't will a pocket of adipose cells into any kind of action. Fat tissue, just like muscle tissue, is anatomically on its own, but it's outside your sphere of control. Nevertheless, the fat tribe is instrumental to your well-being. Fat is a storage device, a kind of biological battery where surplus energy can be stored. As such, some reserve of fat is indispensable for your survival and the survival of your bodily habitat.

As your fat reserves grow, however, you end up with an ever-greater amount of inert body mass that you cannot will into any kind of action. But being the sovereign that you are, you still have to protect, nourish, and feed all of your cellular subjects, including this inert adipose tribe. That's right, fat cells—as any life-forms that are within the dominion of your overall body—require energy themselves. They too get hungry, and they too aspire to live and multiply.

So what you've got in the case of weight gain is the equivalent of a car that's towing an ever-growing gas station of potential fuel. The more weight you gain, the more you change the proportion of functionally controllable tissue to functionally inert tissue. And if you keep gaining weight, you may also begin to lose innervation of muscle tissue due to diabetic neuropathy. The gas station of theoretically usable energy resources keeps growing, but your towing capacity keeps diminishing due to all of the musculoskeletal wear and tear and cardiovascular impairments that undermine neural control.

Viewed as such, obesity is both a loss of self and a gradual loss of control. Indeed, each neuropathic withering reduces the neural tribe that you are, as well as the scope of your dominance over this bodily habitat. When you started on this life trip, you were a muscle car with enough adipose fuel to get you from one meal to another. But if you become morbidly obese, you're more like a quickly deteriorating clunker towing a trailer full of fuel that you really don't need. In a sense, you end up being a needle of control inside a mounting haystack of inertia. Life comes to a standstill. You become both physically and functionally immobile. You find yourself subjectively adrift amidst a hapless mass of body matter that has nothing to do with you. You—the central nervous system plus peripheral nervous system, allied with muscle tissue—find yourself engulfed by an adipose environment that's largely indifferent to your well-being.

You used to rule this land, and now you're an ignored has-been neural monarch. Formerly, if you wanted to go for a walk you would command this body to take you there. Now your body only wants to sit and uses pain and fatigue to blackmail you into submission to its wishes.

Try This: Ditch the BMI for the SMI

Don't let the letters "BMI" worry you. There's nothing to calculate in this meditation; it's just an opportunity to rethink. BMI (body mass index) is a measure of how much of you is fat and how much is muscle. The self mass index (SMI), to coin a metric, is a measure of how much of you is *you* and how much is not-you. Recall that we defined "you" as the neural tribe in charge of the cellular horde of organs, tissues, fat, and fluids attached to a mobile structure of bones. If you are lean and fit, then you—the neural tribe, the mind-side of your distributed neural network—are well represented. There is a lot of your self in this habitat of the body. But if, at the other extreme, you are morbidly obese, then you are like a satellite consulate amidst the land of cellulite: underrepresented, only formally and symbolically in control, and largely overpowered and ignored by the body. In this case, there is far less of you in this cellular environment.

Of course, there is no way of calculating this self mass index. It requires a qualitative kind of self-assessment. To get a sense of your SMI, ask yourself the following questions: "How in control of this body do I feel? How much at home do I feel in this body? Does this body listen to me? Does it obey me, or do I constantly have to compromise and negotiate with it? Does this body feel like mine, or do I feel at the mercy of this body? Who is in charge—me, the neural tribe, or my weight, the adipose tribe? Can I recognize myself in this bodily environment? Does it feel like me? Does this body behave, or does it behave as though I (the neural tribe) don't even matter?" Consider whether you (the neural tribe) feel that you have some clout—some weight, as it were—in this body-land of yours. In short, instead of trying to fit your body into an older pair of jeans, try to make this body-land of yours fit into your existential aspirations. Instead of chasing a sexier BMI, consider focusing on a more sovereign, more representative self mass index. How? Increasing your self-presence through mindful eating will help you increase your sense of neural control in your body.

Try This: Rethink Weight Loss as Self-Gain

Reenvision your weight management goals as self-restoration goals, as a recovery of identity and a return of functional sovereignty to the neural tribe that you are. After all, what really matters about losing weight is not the look of your new waistline but that you—the mind of the matter, the neural tribe—don't have to waste away on the park benches of your body-land. Instead of setting numerical or other quantitative goals, set functional goals, such as being able to tie your shoelaces, get out of your chair without a prop, or walk up a flight of stairs without a respiratory crisis, as well as quality-of-life goals, like "I want to feel in control of my body" or "I want to be able to do the things I want to do." Spend more time with a diary and less time on the scale. Shift your attention from watching your weight drop to watching your self grow.

Try This: Govern the Neural "We"

Nicholas II, the last Russian tsar, was often ridiculed for his use of the royal "we." But I think this kind of language makes sense. A head of state, being the representative of a collective, has to think not of "I" but of "we." The neural tribe that is you is also a head of state, a neural "we" of sorts. Experiment with this neural/royal "we" as you tackle a craving. Next time you find yourself besieged by a craving, climb on the neural throne and try to survey the moment on the behalf of your entire bodily collective. Actually ask yourself, "Do we—the united states of this bodymind—need another cookie?" Before you answer your plural neural self, wield some of your neural powers: Flex each hand into a fist and then release in a demonstration of your neural control over your allied muscle forces. Take a couple of deep, conscious breaths to consult your allied organ forces. Then, after this show of neural force, answer yourself: "No, we don't."

Try This: Prime the Neural Pump

If you wish to skip the royal "we" theatrics, here's a different approach: before you make a decision about whether to overeat or not, flex your consciousness. Move your hand, take a conscious breath, and tap your knee. By engaging in a series of conscious voluntary movements, you give your neural self a chance to step up to the plate. In other words, consciously inhabit your body for a moment or two before you duel with an overeating zombie on autopilot. Consider these moments of mindfulness and presence a way of priming the neural pump.

Conclusion: What's Eating You?

Existentially speaking, obesity is more of a self-management problem than a weight-management problem. While gaining excessive weight or being unable to lose it are understandably frustrating, what's even more existentially disconcerting is the emerging sense of being out of control. This loss of self-control, this sense of being increasingly less in charge of your body, is nothing less than a loss of self, a loss of you. As your control over your body diminishes, so does your sense of self. As you chronically overeat and gain weight, mouthful by mouthful you are literally eating into your sense of self. As your body expands, you—the subjective, psychological self that lives inside your body, the subjective feeling of the neural tribe that is you—diminish in proportion. Putting aside scenarios of so-called infectobesity (where weight gain is thought to be a result of überefficient energy-extracting bacterial gut flora), the issue of weight management is up to you, the neural tribe. After all, there is no eating without your neural say-so. The first step on the journey of recovering your sense of self is reinventing the meal to reinstate yourself as master of your bodily domain—one mindful meal at a time.

An Amuse-Bouche of Pattern Interruption

I hope you've enjoyed these mind teasers. I hope you've begun to develop an appetite for thinking about the mystery of eating before you eat. As you polish off one of the last batches of pattern-interruption amuse-bouches, remember that you can always come back for mind-opening seconds. Reread before you re-eat.

Breathlessness of Eating

We typically don't think of eating as a mechanical threat to our well-being, but with its attendant risks of choking and aspiration, eating is indeed a respiratory risk and can kill you (Sayadi and Herskowitz 2010). But that's old news. Here's something that's hopefully new for you to consider: "During swallowing, you actually stop breathing for a fraction of a second as food travels past the closed entrance to the trachea" (Reader's Digest 2002, 20). Here's another curious fact: it's esti-mated that the average person spends a sum total of five years eating and drinking (Reader's Digest 2002)—and therefore not breathing. When you have a moment, contemplate this: eating is breathlessness. Have a bite of something and watch the wheel of your breath come to a standstill.

Unprocessed Life

In 2009, I read a passage by philosopher Gregory Sams that nearly made me jump out of my chair: "There are a staggering number of edible vegetable combinations of light, air, water, and earth that are growing on this planet. The same base ingredients that produce a carrot can also make a grain of rice or a hot ginger root. The widely different vibrations and life-energies in food are real, and become you if they have not been processed out by the time it reaches your plate. Good food enables and even guides you to live your life much better on many levels—beyond improving simply physical health" (2009, 208–209). For years I have been of the same opinion: that processed food is dead, that the life has been processed out of it, and that it therefore has nothing to offer or teach your bodymind.

It's mind-expanding to see reality through an information-processing lens. But what is information? Information is pattern, and information processing is pattern recognition. Processed food is utterly deconstructed; it has no pattern left. It is sterilized of its history and carries no memory or life secret. An apple is an embryo. It's a vegetative womb pregnant with life. Apple puree is a totally different story. As I see it, even a glass of carrot juice is processed food—even if freshly pressed. Carrot juice is no longer a carrot. Its fibrous structure has been lost in the rpms of a high-powered juicer. Don't get me wrong: I'm not against juicing—not at all. I love carrot juice, and if you see a tan tone to my skin, it's probably attributable to carrots, not sun.

The point I'm making here is philosophical, not nutritional. Whether nutritionally sound or not, processed food is devoid of patterns of information and history. Even if it feeds the body, it doesn't feed the mind. While nutritionally sound processed food is, of course, a better choice than many packaged foods, when I eat it I feel that I miss out on the resistance that unprocessed food puts up. When I take in this nutritional mush, the boa constrictor of my peristalsis has nothing to wrestle with. I yearn for the internal massage of the food as it works its way through me—something that's lost in the flash flood of nutrient flow from processed foods.

The living tube of my body watches all of the food that passes through it, which is perhaps akin to a reality TV show about life outside the body. If the food I eat has had all of its story processed out, it's just pabulum—mush that teaches my body nothing about the dog-eats-dog jungle of life outside its walls. A slice of white bread teaches my body that the outside world is a washed-out sky with an occasional cloud drifting unmemorably past. The roughage of sprouted-grain bread, on the other hand, more accurately conveys the grind of daily life in the outside world. Maybe this is nothing but arbitrary poetics. Maybe nutritional value is, from the body's point of view, the only informational value—but maybe not. In any case, there's no need to tie these loose ends into a tidy knot of facts. All I'm suggesting is that every now and then you welcome an encounter with an actual life-form.

If you're going to have a carrot, have a carrot stick, not carrot juice. If you are going to eat a bird, have an actual chicken leg, not an industrially regurgitated chicken finger. (Just so you know, chickens don't actually have fingers.) And if you're determined to have a glass of orange juice, then at least do the squeezing yourself. Meet what you destroy face-to-face and learn from the encounter. You wouldn't take love in pill form, would you? Of course not. You'd want all the convoluted drama of it: the chase, the challenge, the intimacy of bonding. You'd want the *process* of love. It's the same with food: our bodies want to partake in the digestive process of eating life. Love the unmistakable three-dimensional intimacy of eating an orange, rather than settling for a pale imitation in juice form.

A Diet of Light

Consider this. The ultimate foundation of the food chain is something quite intangible: sunlight. As philosopher Gregory Sams puts it, "Virtually every food we consume, with the exception of salt and some food additives, is a form of stored Sunlight. This is originally laid down as energy through the photosynthesis of plants, and subsequently released as energy to sustain the life of those eating the plants, and those eating those eating the plants, and so on up the food chain" (2009, 207). As you eat your next meal, ask yourself, "How enlightened is my diet—literally? How close am I to the primordial source of energy? Am I getting fresh, relatively unfiltered light energy, or the tired hand-me-downs—the products of other beings' recycling?" Just because you sit at the top of the solar-powered food-chain doesn't necessarily mean you're getting top-shelf energy. Look at a five-thousand-year-old sequoia and then look at yourself. Tell me: who's eating better?

Food Addiction? Nah!

Some people beat themselves up with the label "food addict," which can reinforce the idea that they "just can't stop eating." I don't buy it. In the 1983 book *Chocolate to Morphine: Understanding Mind-Active Drugs*, Andrew Weil and Winifred Rosen place chocolate and morphine into one and the same broad category—drugs—explaining that humans have a seemingly innate interest in altering their consciousness. Naturally, chocolate and morphine are in different leagues. But the principle nevertheless holds: anything you eat for pleasure alters your consciousness from a baseline of boredom to a more pleasurable or stimulated state.

In any case, ditch the word "addiction" from your vocabulary. It means nothing. Whether you are "addicted" to morphine or to tiramisu, at a motivational level you're a pleasure seeker. And there is nothing fundamentally wrong with seeking pleasure. The path we take on this journey in search of pleasure can certainly be more or less precarious. It can be legal or illegal, socially sanctioned or stigmatizing, but the destination is always the same: pleasure, which is a form of well-being. If you've labeled yourself as a food addict, I suggest you retire this psychologically toxic concept from your mind. You're a seeker of well-being who is still mastering the learning curve of moderation.

Share your mindful eating experiences online using the Mindful Eating Tracker at http://www.eatingthemoment.com/mindfulness-tracker.

chapter 12

Reinventing the
Iconography of Eating

Enjoy your food, but eat less.

— U.S. Department of Agriculture

There are sobering realizations that you cannot, unfortunately, unthink. Here's one such realization that I had a few years back: health, unlike illness, produces no revenue. That's right: in economic terms, you are far more valuable sick than healthy. Healthy bodies with healthy minds make for poor consumers in a corporate society. They mind their own business and live their lives of quiet satisfaction. The ill, however, are understandably busy looking for either direct or symbolic answers to their suffering. That makes them excellent consumers. Illness is a repeat business. Health, sales-wise, is a cold lead. It's easy to dismiss this perspective as depressing or unnecessarily cynical. But I encourage you to not rush to brush this off as a disillusioning rant by some weirdo. Granted, I might be a weirdo, but as for disillusionment, it's always a good thing. Disillusionment is literally a loss of illusion, and is therefore an opportunity to see reality as it is. It's an opportunity for clarity—an opportunity for change.

Mindfulness Is the Missing Ingredient

Let us start with a brief review before I make my point: Eating changes both body and mind, the totality of who we are. What we eat and how much we eat changes who we are physiologically. Why we eat and how we eat changes who we are psychologically.

Mindlessness Is Blindness

When we eat mindlessly, the body expands (to the extent that mindless eating leads to overeating) and the mind shrinks (to the extent that mindless eating denies us the experience of eating). After all, being mindless means just that: being of less mind. Mindlessness hides reality and robs us of experience. I'm sure you're familiar with this experience of having no experience: You get into the car, start driving, and half an hour later arrive at your destination. But as you look back, you don't remember the actual experience of driving. We've learned not to be puzzled by that. "Highway hypnosis," we think, and move on. It's the same with eating—a kitchen-table hypnosis of sorts. You shop, you cook, you set up the meal, you turn on the TV, and several mindless minutes later you're done. Your stomach is full but your mind is empty, and you're craving seconds just so you can have the experience of eating that you missed the first time around.

Mindfulness Is Vision

When we eat mindfully, the body shrinks (to the extent that mindful eating reduces mindless overeating) and the mind expands. After all, being mindful means just that: having a full mind. Mindfulness is vision. Mindfulness reveals the reality of what is, in all its nuanced, complex, and unique suchness. The tradition of saying grace to infuse a moment of spiritual gratitude into a meal; the Zen tradition of *oryoki*, which facilitates here-and-now presence through meditative eating; the veganism movement, with its attempt to manifest the ethics of compassion through eating—these and many other food-related traditions all reflect that eating can serve as an invaluable existential platform for awakening the zombie in us. Whereas mindless eating robs us of the eating moments of our lives, mindful eating allows us to reclaim those experiences. According to the website of the Center for Mindful Eating (2011), "Mindful eating has the powerful potential to transform people's relationship to food and eating [and] to improve overall health, body image, relationships, and self-esteem." Recent years have witnessed the emergence of self-help and clinical literature on mindfulness-based counseling for overeating and binge-eating. The conclusion that has become increasingly clear is simply this: mindful eating is an essential part of healthy eating.

An Icon of the Past

For years, the USDA food pyramid was a cultural icon. It was designed to guide our eating behavior, yet mindful eating was conspicuously absent. As a case in point, the final version of the food pyramid featured a human figure flying up a set of stairs to indicate the importance of exercise. Great idea, except…the runner's head was disconnected from its body, just like so much of our eating behavior is disconnected from our mind's conscious intent. In a 2010 post in my Huffington Post blog, I called on the USDA to update the food pyramid. At that time I proposed that, at a minimum, we'd do well to connect the runner's mind to his or her body by adding a neck to unite the parts of the human whole. But I didn't stop there. I also suggested that we crown the pyramid with a symbol of mindfulness—namely, an eye symbol like that on the back of a dollar bill. My thinking was that this addition would cue people to the importance of eating with both short- and long-term vision: with here-and-now tactical awareness of the process of eating and with strategic vision about how one's eating behavior fits with one's overall philosophy about how to live.

The symbol of the all-seeing eye at the top of a pyramid, by the way, traces its origin back to ancient Egypt and indicates "that the dead god is entombed in the underworld but is still watchful. The open eye is his soul that is still alive, so he knows what is happening in the world" (Forty 2003, 11). Because this symbol appears on the dollar bill and has become largely accepted as a legitimate part of American iconography, I felt it had been sufficiently secularized that it might also appear atop the food pyramid.

The Icon of the Present

The food pyramid was, in fact, changed. But not in the manner I had petitioned for. As you probably know, the food pyramid has been bull-dozed down for good. The new USDA visual guide to healthful eating is a colorful plate of fruits, veggies, protein, and grain on what looks like a cafeteria-style food tray, with a side of dairy. This is a genuine improvement over the food pyramid. First of all, a plate of food on a tray is far more intuitive and face valid than a food pyramid.

Furthermore, the USDA plate (2011) doesn't just tell us what to eat and how much to eat ("eat less"), it also gives us a glimpse of *how* to eat. To the left of the plate, there is a fork. I guess we are being asked to use utensils rather than eat with our hands. Okay, I'm being snarky. The old issue remains: There is no visual cue for mindful eating. Admittedly, the text that goes with the plate advocates that you "enjoy your food." But it seems most of us are already quite adept at this. If that's USDA-speak for conscious eating, I think it's a bit too cryptic. In my view, this ostensibly fresh, new USDA icon is already outdated. Perhaps they are still climbing that ancient pyramid of learning.

Therefore, my proposal remains the same: we need to add an explicit visual icon for mindfulness—perhaps a pair of glasses in which one lens reads "mindful" and the other reads "eating," or a lotus flower with the inscription "Eating is yoga." Seriously though, I'm not a graphic designer and this isn't a fine arts dissertation. It's a platform for posing a rhetorical question to the USDA think tank: Don't you see that as an (over)eating civilization we need some kind of visual cue for the idea that mindlessness is blindness and mindfulness is vision?

Conclusion: A Do-It-Yourself Project

Eating is physiologically inevitable, but mindfulness isn't. Associating eating with mindfulness, one meal at a time, can not only help us manage weight (by reducing mindless overeating), it can also nourish and enrich the mind. Of course, you don't have to wait for the USDA to update the iconography of recommended eating. You can do it yourself. Just add the missing ingredient of mindfulness to round out your meals.

In this day and age of nationwide emphasis on battling the epidemic of obesity, reconfiguring the USDA's food-related iconography to reflect the importance of mindfulness in eating would seem to be a pretty simple and obvious step. But I guess nothing is simple enough for the government heads that are largely disconnected from the body politic. For the time being, mindful eating remains a do-it-yourself project. This is fine. All breakthroughs of the spirit and mind are, ultimately, self-governed endeavors anyway. The time to start is now. As for the iconography of eating, hopefully the imagery of the future will one day reflect (rather than solely advise) the eating psychology of a conscious nation.

An Amuse-Bouche of Pattern Interruption

There is no reinvention without rethinking. And there is no rethinking without thinking. To reinvent the meal, you have to rethink the meal. To rethink the meal, you have to think about eating. No, not when you eat. When you eat, just eat. Think *before* you eat. Start now.

To Eat Is to Touch Is to Change

In *Living Across and Through Skins*, feminist philosopher Sharon Sullivan wrote, "As an organ...skin is more than mere boundary. It functions as the site of transaction between inside and outside the body" (2001, 158). To eat is to touch. But to touch is also to change. Indeed, eating, as touch, is a two-way transaction: we change that which we eat, and we transform ourselves through the process of eating. At your next meal, recognize that as you touch, you are touched, and that as you change, you are changed.

Eating Is Rebirth

To eat is to re-create yourself—literally, not metaphorically. Each meal is the beginning of a rebirth. The you that you currently are is about to die as you replace yourself with a new you that you are about to create with the help of what you are eating. The wheel of eating is the wheel of rebirth. As you sit down to your next meal, recognize yourself as your own creator. Feel the freedom and the responsibility that come with this act of eating re-creation/recreation.

Dao Food

Deng Ming-Dao wrote, "If you give the masters something to eat, they will eat. If they have nothing to eat, they forget that there was ever such an activity" (1992, 224). Hmm. Masters of what? They must be masters of self. Hmm. Why would a master of self be so nonchalant about eating? Must be already full, I suspect. Full of what? That's for you to figure out. Here are your choices:

a. Full of self

b. Full of emptiness

c. Full of Dao

d. All of the above (are the same)

A Namaste of Metabolic Interdependence

All life distinguishes "inside" from "outside," or "self" from "nonself." This is the fundamental duality, distinction, bias, or sapience/wisdom that all life operates on. Life is self-serving and partial to self. It views its own self as the subject and everything else as "other," "environment," or "objects." All life objectifies other life as "environment," to use and to eat, to flee from so as to not be used or eaten by it, or both. All life is fundamentally unfair to other life—until it understands its inevitable interdependence and, on a higher level, its essential sameness.

Early in our development—both as individuals and as cultures—we adopt an adaptively intense dualism of self and nonself. We are highly self-centered (egocentric). It makes sense. Being helpless and scared, we have to think in a highly conservative manner. This developmentally early dualism is there to protect us. "You're either with me or against me" is the mentality that underlies our socializing. We socialize not for fun but for protection. We group into cliques and circle the wagons. We are busy surviving.

As we learn more about life, we begin to tame our fears and distinguish between physical and symbolic threats. If we're fortunate, we eventually conquer our innermost fear: the fear of dying. As we progress from fear to nonfear, we become increasingly less invested in all of these us-versus-them distinctions. The lens of our perception is recalibrated to notice similarity, perhaps even the oneness of our shared essence, rather than superficial differences in form. We become kinder and more compassionate. We even begin to feel for the life that we consume each time we sit down to eat—not just the animals that died so we might mindlessly eat another meal while zoned out in front of the TV, but even the plant-based life we consume. We begin to get it that anything that is alive wants to stay alive, regardless of its level of complexity.

A sense of tender intimacy emerges as we eat—not guilt that we have to consume something living in order to live, but a sense of interconnectedness, a realization that as we eat this Earth, we become this Earth, that as we eat this food, we become future food. This creates a kind of camaraderie of existence: a baseline sympathy, a gradual but never complete dissolution of subject-object duality, a universal willingness to relate, to feel for the other—kindness, if you will. So how does eating come into this? Eating is a reunion of self and nonself, of me and not-me, of you and not-you, of eater and food through the enmeshment of eating. Eating is twofold yoga: a yoga that unifies your body with your mind, and, at a higher level, a yoga that unifies you with your environment. An eating moment is a bittersweet moment of connection—a namaste of metabolic interdependence.

Trinity of a Meal

There is you, the eater, there is food, and there is the process of eating. Eater, food, eating—I think of this as the trinity of the meal. All three of these aspects require attention. Throughout, the goal of this book has been to help you reconnect with your body, with your mind, and with the world. This too is a trinity of the meal—just stated differently. (My use of the word "trinity" here isn't intended to offend any spiritual sensibilities; on the contrary, the intent is to encourage them.)

I recently heard a comedian quote Mike Tyson as saying, "Everyone has a plan until you punch them in the face." Having grown up with a father whose first ghostwriting projects were on behalf of such Soviet boxing stars as Valeri Popenchenko and Algirdas Shotsikas, I got my fair share of streetwise advice, and it usually involved pattern interruption—meaning an unexpected move. That's what these sections were intended to do: knock out your preconceived notions about eating. I've seen this plan—the plan of pattern interruption—at work in my middle school brawls, in the workings of psychology, and in life in general. Sure, my provocations are not invulnerable to deep analysis. And you can easily find some inconsistencies of position. That's fine. After all, my goal isn't to make sense per se, but to toss a monkey wrench into the wheel-like pattern of your thoughts about eating and thereby help you open your mind before you open your mouth.

I hope I succeeded. This was necessary. Instead of cleaning your plate, you need to clean the cobwebs of eating orthodoxy out of your mind. My guess is that you will never think of eating in the same way again, and that's what matters. After all, until the rug of familiar beliefs has been pulled from underneath your feet, how are you to enjoy a picnic of mindfulness in the lush lap of Mother Nature? I can almost hear a tired, exasperated gasp from you, dear reader: "What's this metaphorical nonsense he's spewing out again?!" Nothing, fellow mind, nothing. Just a parting jab on the chin of your dualistic logic. Well, I do have one last trick up my sleeve. Read on.

Share your mindful eating experiences online using the Mindful Eating Tracker at http://www.eatingthemoment.com/mindfulness-tracker.

chapter 13

Reinventing the Species

*Life is the transmutation of energy and matter. Solar fire
transmutes into the green fire of photosynthetic beings. Green fire
transmutes to the red and orange and yellow and purple sexual
fire of flowering plants... Fossilized green fire is hoarded in the
human cubicle of solar economy... A transhuman being,
superhumanity is appearing, becoming part of the sentient
symphony... Life today is an autopoietic, photosynthetic
phenomenon, planetary in scale. A chemical transmutation
of sunlight, it exuberantly tries to spread, to outgrow itself.*

— Lynn Margulis and Dorion Sagan, *What Is Life?*

Carl Jung once said, "As far as we can discern, the sole purpose of
human existence is to kindle a light in the darkness of mere being"
(1963, 326). Was Jung being literal or metaphorical when he wrote this?
Was this image of light a metaphor for mindfulness, or was he talking
about something even deeper? Who knows! In any case, Jung's thought
about kindling a light—along with similar thoughts by others—has
long set my curiosity on fire. Everything we eat is trickle-down solar
energy. In a manner of speaking, we eat light.

This chapter is about the possibility of truly enlightened eating. And when I say "enlightened eating," I mean it literally. Could we literally live off light? Is human photosynthesis a possibility? Whether you see this line of inquiry as mystical lyricism, science fiction, or a legitimate scientific prospect is a litmus test of your views about the nature of life, and human life in particular. The goal of this chapter is to envision a solution to the heterotroph's dilemma of having to kill for sustenance. Whereas mindful eating is about eating more humanely (in relationship to both self and others), the idea of human photosynthesis is fundamentally transhuman. So hold on to your hat as we explore the possibility of reinventing our species by reinventing our relationship to light. Literally.

The Samsara of Heterotrophy

As I shared in the introduction to this book, my dad once mused, "Nobody invented the wheel! It just rolled into our lives all by itself." While to this day I am not sure if he was being literal or metaphorical, I myself now know what wheel keeps us going: the wheel of eating. Buddhists speak of samsara, or the wheel of suffering—a kind of hellish merry-go-around of transmutation as we try to pay down our karmic mortgage. While I don't believe in reincarnation in a literal sense, we are certainly continuously dying and being reborn. We are constantly renewing ourselves with each metabolic exchange, with each breath we take, and with each life we take to feed ourselves. In my view, life is a nonstop ceasing and arising, a continuous metabolic death and rebirth. As such, life is a wheel. According to the Buddhist worldview, this wheel of samsara is fueled by desire. Suffering (*dukkha* in Pali) is a function of thirst (*tanha* in Pali). *Tanha* is a kind of existential thirst: an incessant desire, searching, restlessness, and dissatisfaction and a constant desire to optimize.

This thirst is the very motion of the wheel of suffering. Without motion, there is no wheel. Without searching, there is no dissatisfaction. Thus, the wheel of suffering is, paradoxically, fueled by our relentless pursuit of well-being. We always want more and therefore never feel like we have enough. This is our psychological hell. As we try to claw out of it, we keep consuming lives, keep killing to live, and, as a result, keep running up our karmic debt. So we keep coming back, reincarnating (literally or metaphorically), time after time after time to pay the debt down through good merit, compassion, and loving-kindness. To reincarnate is simply to reembody this endless thirst into yet another body of yearning. The Buddhist treatment plan for this carousel of suffering is to let go of desire, to get off the merry-go-round of zero-sum living. How? Through mindful living.

Two Metabolic Routes, Two Karmic Paths

The wheel of samsara is the wheel of eating is the wheel of killing is the wheel of suffering is the wheel of living at others' expense is the wheel of heterotrophy. Life on Earth knows two ways: to live off the sun or to live off each other. As discussed previously, plant life is autotrophic, that is, nutritionally self-sufficient. Animals—humans included—are parasitic, predatory, and zero-sum (and I say that lovingly, because we are what we are, nothing more and nothing less). We are heterotrophs. We eat others. We eat autotrophs (plant life) and other heterotrophs. The very dilemma of our existence is that we have to kill to live; we have to destroy to eat. That's bad karma.

With the notable exception of a few carnivorous species, plants kill nothing. They feed off the sun. Their karmic bill of health is pristine. Animals, on the other hand, had to evolve a locomotion system to move from famine to food, and from being food to procuring food. To further fine-tune this procurement project, animals had to evolve a nervous system to improve their control of their locomotive apparatus, to better navigate from famine to food, and from being food to turning other beings into food.

Unlike plants, animals are always in search. Instead of accepting the reality of what is environmentally given, animals are chronically caught up in the process of optimizing their well-being. In sum, as animals we are stuck on an existential hamster wheel, ever restless and caught up in the samsara of eating.

Plants, on the other hand, live a monklike existence of graceful acceptance. They are literally and metaphorically rooted and grounded in whatever metabolic circumstances they find themselves in. They neither search nor thirst. They need not meditate; they are already in lifelong *zazen*. They stay put, rushing nowhere, yearning for nothing, busy with nothing, and growing effortlessly. If you ask me, any blade of grass has more equanimity than the Dalai Lama. Plant life is utterly non-neurotic because it has no need for the nervous system that enables such a state. Plants are life at its most unencumbered—literally enlightened living. So if you ever wanted to shake hands with the Dalai Lama, try hugging a tree.

Try This: Fan the Green Coals

Let's pause for a moment of contemplation about something seemingly mundane and innocently routine: grocery shopping. Every so often, we buy a shopping cart of destruction. This isn't a guilt trip; it's just a reality check. Each act of purchasing today ensures that tomorrow more carrots will be yanked out of the soil and more lobsters will be boiled. Putting aside the question of whether there is really such a thing as the humane murder of an unwilling living victim, destruction is destruction. This is our heterotrophic predicament, and grocery shopping is how we give momentum to this samsaric merry-go-round of zero-sum living, with the help of our dollars, rubles, euros, yuans, rupees, and tugriks.

There are no autotrophic options available to us just yet. But here's what I'd like for you to do. Next time you shop for groceries, pause in the produce isle and take a long, enchanted look at the fruits and vegetables that killed no one and yet are in a position to feed you. Take a similarly long, ponderous look at the grains and nuts that are soon to share their stored sun energy with you. See if you can turn the samsara of grocery shopping into a moment of admiration for the green coals that fuel our existential fire.

Try This: Track the Light

Recall that all energy on this planet is, in one way or another, a product of the sun. As you fill up your shopping cart the next time you buy groceries, try to mentally track the connection between any given foodstuff and the sun. Plants are, of course, easy. It's nearly automatic to envision them outside, basking in the sun and soaking up the energy of light. With animal products it's a bit harder. Something like protein powder is even more obscure. Try nevertheless. Retrace the steps of the biochemical metamorphosis: The planet turns, light hits a sprouting blade of grass, the grass grows tall enough to be noticed by the mowing jaws of a grazing calf, the calf grows into a cow, the cow becomes a number of steaks, the steaks become your body, and your body fuels your mind as you think this very thought. Bam! The energy of light has finally reached you. Feel the touch of the sun as your consciousness ponders your own connection to it. Track the light in your food for a bit of self-illumination.

There Are No Metabolic Saints

I am not a druid or a tree hugger, although I have certainly hugged a few trees. I don't worship trees. I'm well aware of the fact that plant life isn't entirely karmically innocent. Yes, there are carnivorous plants, and there are numerous plants species that have given up their capacity for photosynthesis and instead steal sustenance from fellow plants. I have no doubt that if plant life had its survival challenged by chronically low light conditions, it would eventually find a way to do what heterotrophs do: consume others' energy supplies. This isn't surprising. The precedents of heterotrophic behavior among plants are already there. Ultimately, all life—at its core—is zero-sum. Life is fundamentally self-perpetuating, self-maintaining, and self-nurturing, that is, egocentric and self-serving. To live you have take something. Plants and trees aren't metabolic saints, they've just found a way to get by on far less than we do. They eat photons, air, water, and minerals—presumably inanimate elements of nature, not subject to suffering. But who knows, maybe even light hurts when metabolized into energy. I can't be sure. Can you?

Ideas, Anyone?

While literally enlightened living—living without the necessity of killing—sounds karmically or ethically appealing, I don't want to be a vegetable. And yet the heterotrophic eating lifestyle is eating at many of us. Here lies the heterotroph's dilemma: to kill to eat is so human, and yet it feels so inhumane. What are we to do? Devolution is not an option. Evolutionary processes take too long. However, transhuman engineering does seem like a theoretically viable option. The idea isn't as crazy as it sounds. Many people—mystics, scientists, and transhumanists—have already mused about the possibility of living off light directly.

Mani's Enlightenment

Mani, the founder of Manichaeanism, born in Persia in 216 CE, tried to get off the samsaric wheel of zero-sum living by eating light, literally. According to polymath Colin Spencer in his book *The Heretic's Feast* (1996), Mani learned about vegetarianism from members of the Elcesaites, a religious sect that "celebrated the Eucharist with unleavened bread and water and washed themselves and their food according to certain rules of purity" (136). The Elcesaites believed that "all defilement is from the body...you yourselves are clothed in" (137). This notion gave Mani his ideological blueprint for dividing the world into two substances—matter and soul (spirit or consciousness)—and positing that soul substance is trapped in matter substance. This was the basis of his unqualified compassion for all living forms. Mani had visions and believed that he had a "divine twin, an emanation of the Jesus of Light that gave him guidance" (137). By the standards of official Christendom, Mani was a dangerous heretic. But that's not the point.

What's of interest is his attempt to overcome heterotrophy. By recognizing the soul in all that's living, by believing that all living life is sentient, Mani, like Jainists, felt compassion for other life-forms.

Already a vegetarian, "he did not wish to harvest the fruit and vegetables himself, but only to accept them as alms... Blood, he claimed, oozed from the places where the plants had been hurt by the sickle: the vegetable world cried out with a human voice at the pain it received. When taken by force to pick dates, the tree spoke to Mani calling him a murderer" (137). Whether Mani was highly empathic or psychotic—or both—is irrelevant. What matters is that he had a point. Modern-day science does support the notion that plants have inner life. And why wouldn't they? They are alive, after all. All life—at its core—is responsive to stimuli and has a desire for self-preservation.

Mani's "heretic" diet resulted in his premature demise. He was tortured to death by the Christian establishment. But his eating philosophy also earned him a powerful following that outlived many contemporary "heretical" teachings and persisted for seven centuries, taking root in distant lands, including China. "Mani was a visionary, poet, artist and missionary," with a theology of "startling originality" (138). He believed that "there is a divine spark buried in the matter of this world, encased in the flesh of the body" (138), and he tried to liberate this spark by eating light in the form of light particles that had been amassed by fruits and vegetables that—in their autotrophic eating style—are closer to the light (sun) than we, the heterotrophs.

Mani's followers observed the so-called Seal of the Mouth, which forbade consumption of meat since "meat contained fewer light particles than plants, because animals fed off the plants and some of the light which they had ingested escaped" (139). As you see, Mani, with a good degree of rationality and common sense, believed that light is divine (and after all, it does literally support all living activity on this planet); and that plants consume light, which makes them somewhat holy; and that if one wishes to get more enlightened, one needs to consume more light in the form of plant-based light particles.

But, of course, Mani's take was more religion than science. His followers were divided into the Elect and the Auditors (the Hearers). The Elect, by abstaining from meat, consumed more light, and it was their job to release these light particles through...belching. That's right. And just like many before him, Mani believed in reincarnation. The Elect, being "souls already suffused with light" (141), having literally enlightened themselves by eating light, were nirvanically released into the Kingdom of Light, while the Hearers "underwent a series of reincarnations in the bodies of fruits and vegetables and eventually into the Elect themselves" (140–141).

Holy Cow!

Mani's experiment makes a certain amount of sense. Recall the commonly accepted dictum "You are what you eat." If this idea has merit, it holds that merit for all beings. What do plants eat? Mostly light. So if plants are what they eat, they are mostly light. What about heterotrophs? The vegan and vegetarian heterotrophs mostly eat plants that are mostly light. Therefore, a plant-eating heterotroph, such as a cow, is a bit more full of light (more sacred, more enlightened) than a cow-eating wolf. Holy cow! Mani might have had a point. Don't worry; I'm not trying to insinuate some kind ethical superiority about the virtues of veganism or vegetarianism. I don't consider vegans and vegetarians any holier than carnivores and omnivores.

Fantasies of Energy Independence

As Colin Spencer observed, "In Manichaeanism, for the first time, we see a new and quite different reason for the abstention from meat. Compared to the Pythagorean dogma which entails respect for another living creature because it contains a living soul, the Manichean [reason is that] partaking of flesh will weigh the spirit down... Eat meat and you will trap the spirit in more flesh" (144). I think Mani was motivated by a variety of sentiments. Formally and officially, he was motivated by the pursuit of spiritual well-being and purity. I would posit that, psychologically, he was simply overwhelmed with intense empathic identification with all living beings and wished to find a way to minimize the suffering of all living beings. And on a more global level, I think that he, like all life, might have wanted to figure out a way to be metabolically independent. After all, independence is when you need nothing from the environment. Release from the wheel of eating is freedom from dependence on the environment. But from this standpoint, no living entity is free. As enlightened as plants might be, they too are dependent on the environment. After all, a dependence on sunlight, air, water, and the minerals in soil is still a dependence. The life of a plant—while free of killing—is far from energy sovereignty.

Mani—The First Transhumanist

Mani also wanted to transcend a self-imposed mind-made dualism. He wished to free mind (light, spirit, soul, consciousness) from body (matter) because he believed that mind and body were two separate substances. As I see it, this is classic dualistic folly. Your consciousness isn't trapped in the matter of your body. Your consciousness (spirit, soul, mind) is an inner dimension of the material body that you are; that is, it is the subjectivity of the object. As such, there is no soul hostage to liberate. Mani, as I see it, got stuck in chasing the tail of his own conceptual abstraction. He was trying to let a stone out of a stone. It can't be done. We are living, conscious, breathing matter. And we are liquid, feeling, sensing, suffering collections of minerals (a Vernadskian view that I share). No surprise here: being made of the rock called Earth, we are nothing more and nothing less than this rock.

But Mani's experiment wasn't in vain. He reconceptualized spiritual enlightenment and illumination in a most literal way: by encouraging us to eat more light and aspire to be light producing and light emitting. He challenged humanity to find a way to eat the way plants eat and to share the luminescence—a noble, compassionate, and humane goal and, arguably, the first transhuman goal on record. Rest in peace, Persian dreamer, perhaps somewhere in the belly-trunk of a baobab tree or in the opening of a lotus blossom.

Try This: Plug In to the Sun

Vitamin D provides a fascinating metabolic precedent for the possibility of developing plantlike capabilities. As you probably know, we humans can manufacture our own vitamin D merely by exposing our skin to sunlight. Vitamin D is no trivial supplement. It's "a major player in a team of nutrients and hormones" that keeps the human body functioning (Davis and Melina 2000, 133). Why am I all agog about this? We walking trees haven't evolutionarily walked too impossibly far away from our plant kin. We can still photosynthesize! "Big deal," you might say. You might even add, "Just because we can photosynthesize vitamin D doesn't mean we can actually live off sunlight." Maybe not yet—but quite possibly we will be able to someday. For the time being, step out into the sun for a moment or two when you get a chance—maybe even right now. Face the light. Plug into it metabolically if only for the vitamin D (for now). Not for the tan, of course, but for the tantalizing taste of metabolic independence that it offers.

Transhuman Fermentation

Still a cultural underground, transhumanism is a gradual churning of techno-genetic possibilities. As a social movement, transhumanism is still in the stages of fermentation. From the evolutionary standpoint, transhumanism is an attempt at self-guided evolution, a project of customizing the body to meet the needs of the mind. But what does the mind fundamentally need from the body? Faster information processing would be nice. An extended health span would be nifty. Who wouldn't like faster legs, sharper vision, or more acute hearing? Heck, having a functional pair of wings wouldn't hurt either. Top all of this off with bulletproof skin, and it might seem as though this human dream of functional augmentation was complete. But it isn't. It's lacking the most fundamental piece: greater metabolic independence. Indeed, what minds seem to really like is sovereignty. And sovereignty is synonymous with greater energy independence. Of course, all metabolic independence is relative. No life is ultimately independent of its environment.

As I see it, a transhuman project of metabolic independence could take one of two general paths: that of direct human photosynthesis at a cellular level (let's call it the path of *Homo solaris*) or the path of the Energizer Bunny. The former is a path of genetic modification and perhaps surgical augmentation or a wholesale nanosurgical alteration on a cellular level. The latter path might involve some sort of "future skin," a kind of biotech chimera project of swapping elastic solar panels for patches of skin. The specifics are beyond me. In fact, it's likely that there are solutions that lie beyond the capacity of my imagination. But one thing seems clear to me: whether motivated by compassion or self-determination, we will—if we are fortunate to survive as a civilization—seek greater energy autonomy on an individual basis.

There can be a tendency to see transhumanism as a loss of humanity. It certainly may be. But it's also possible to view transhumanism as an amplification of humanity—as the extension of our essence and a liberation of what is best in us from our evolutionary luggage. Understand that change in form is not the same as change in essence. You—the very you that is reading this—have never even been the same as yourself. You are evolving with each left-to-right scan of your eyes, with each inhalation of new air, with each exposure to new information. You are a being in progress, transcending your human form with each pound you gain or lose, with each haircut, and with each new gray hair, yet you remain forever human in your essence. As I see it, we need not fear evolution, whether it occurs naturally or through self-design.

Life Reinvents Itself

In his book *Biospheres*, Dorion Sagan said, "We ourselves are a technology" (1990, 129). Life is a process of constant reinvention. And life is reinventing photosynthesis as we speak. Russian microbiologists Ekaterina Dadachova and Arturo Casadevall (2008) discovered a slime (a fungus) inside the tomb of the Chernobyl reactor that has developed the ability to turn gamma radiation into a food source. World Time News Report (2007) reported:

The fungi appear to use melanin, a chemical found in human skin as well, in the same fashion that plants use chlorophyll. Casadevall and his co-researchers then set about performing a variety of tests... 'Just as the pigment chlorophyll converts sunlight into chemical energy that allows green plants to live and grow, our research suggests that melanin can use a different portion of the electromagnetic spectrum—ionizing radiation—to benefit the fungi containing it,' said co-researcher Ekaterina Dadachova. Interestingly, the melanin in fungi is no different chemically from the melanin in our skin, leading Casadevall to speculate that melanin could be providing energy to skin cells.

Life is reinventing itself not just in the fungi kingdom but right in our relatives in the animal kingdom. In fact, Lynn Margulis and Dorion Sagan reported that several animal species have acquired the ability to photosynthesize, including some species of sea slugs (2002, 13):

> Slugs, the familiar shell-less mollusks eating your garden plants, have entirely green photosynthetic relatives. The ancestors of these slugs have eaten but not digested certain green algae, which years ago entered the tissues of the animal—and stayed there. All members of these species (for example *Elysia viridis*) are always green. These underwater slugs need not seek food. Rather they crawl near the shore. They never eat throughout their adult life. The slugs, newly evolved green animals, now sunbathe in the way plants sunbathe… At least four or five times different lineages of green animals have been documented in videos and scientific papers.

Homo photosyntheticus: Beyond Mouth

As we contemplate human photosynthesis, realize that we are not discussing the future; we're discussing our past. Life has invented photosynthesis not once, but many, many times. Photosynthesis is in life's memory banks. We simply need to find a way to genetically recall this forgotten metabolic secret. Chances are it won't come through meditative insight (although such cases have been claimed). It's more likely that we'll have to swallow some kind of pill or a handful of self-replicating nanorobots that will allow our melanin to function like energy-producing chlorophyll, one cell at a time. And it may be centuries, if not millennia, before we can equip humans with photosynthesis.

But the point is, it seems at least theoretically possible. If life on the order of fungi can figure out how to live off radiation using nothing more than the intelligence of its genes, why can't we? There's no reason why we can't. How can I claim that? Once again, life has done and is doing this, and we are...life. We are the very technology of evolution, self-growth, and self-improvement. As life, we are literally in the business of change. In the lingo of anthropologists, "techno-organic evolution" is upon us (Schick and Toth 1993, 314).

Centuries have passed since the days of Mani, but the meme of human photosynthesis hasn't vanished. Let's take a look at what I call the Margulis-Sagan vision of *Homo photosyntheticus*. Who are these two, whom I've quoted so often throughout this book? Lynn Margulis, a noted biologist, was a distinguished professor in the Department of Geosciences at the University of Massachusetts at Amherst, and the recipient of the 1999 National Medal of Science. She authored more than a hundred articles and a dozen books. Dorion Sagan, the son of Lynn Margulis and astrophysicist Carl Sagan, is a noted science writer who has authored or coauthored over twenty books and received awards for excellence in journalism. Hopefully these credentials will assure you that the ideas they offer are more than flights of fantasy. Here are a couple of excerpts from this dynamic thinking duo on the topic of human photosynthesis. Mind you, theirs is kind of a tongue-in-cheek vision, but, considering the source, it bears consideration (2007, 99):

> Future humans may even be green, a product of symbiosis...
> Evolution has already witnessed nutritional alliances between
> hungry organisms and sunlit, self-sufficient bacteria or algae.
> *Mastigias*, a Pacific Ocean medusoid...helps its photosynthetic
> partners by swimming toward the areas of most intense light.
> They, in return, keep it well fed. This could happen to our
> *Homo photosyntheticus*, a sort of ultimate vegetarian who no
> longer eats but lives on internally produced food from his scalp
> algae. Our *Homo photosyntheticus* descendants might, with
> time, tend to lose their mouths, becoming translucent, slothish,
> and sedentary. Symbiotic [photosynthesizing] algae of *Homo
> photosyntheticus* might eventually find their way to the human
> germ cells. They would first invade testes and from there enter
> sperm cells as they are made... Accompanying the sperm

during mating, and maybe even entering women's eggs, the algae—like a benevolent venereal disease—could ensure their survival in the warm, moist tissues of humans.

What is significant here is that the greening of humans might not have to be accomplished surgically. It might proceed as a form of naturally occurring symbiotic evolution. However, assuming that *Homo photosyntheticus* is indeed an eventual possibility, the species need not lose its mouth. Given that in that distant future we'll probably still need mouths to communicate, we can always keep them functioning with chewing gum. We also need not be slothful or sedentary, as Margulis and Sagan envision. Bamboo—powered by nothing but photosynthesis—has been documented to surge skyward as fast as almost forty inches in a twenty-four-hour period. Surely we can learn to dial our intensity up and down as needed.

In continuing to lay out the possibilities, Margulis and Sagan said, "We can imagine ourselves as future forms of prosthetically pared people—with perhaps only our delicately dissected nervous systems attached to electronically driven plastic limbs and levers—lending decision-making power to the maintenance functions of reproducing spacecraft" (100). This may sound like science fiction, but it isn't. Recall the discussion of obesity in chapter 11. In a most basic sense, we are not our bodies; we are the distributed neural network that runs the biological machinery of locomotion and energy production.

The vision of "delicately dissected nervous systems" that are "prosthetically pared" to lend decision-making power to machinery is already in the process of becoming reality. Recent medical developments, arising particularly from military medicine and bordering on augmentation, have made remarkable advances in bridging the technological and neural. We have already learned to connect wires and nerves. If we imagine ourselves as nervous systems wired into machinery with photoelectric power supplies, we are seeing a cyborglike vision of *Homo photosyntheticus*. Whether this is more or less humane depends not on the form that we assume but on how we utilize our essence—how we apply our humanity.

Ask most people about what or who they are at their core, and you'll probably hear such words as "spirit," "consciousness," and "energy." When you strip yourself away from inconsequential roles and circumstances and look at the ground of your being, you don't really see flesh; what you see is an ephemeral self-awareness, a nebula of presence, perhaps a light of awareness. Being made of stars, it's no wonder that our essence shines from within us. As Transcendentalist Ralph Waldo Emerson noted, "From within or from behind, a light shines through us upon things, and makes us aware that we are nothing, but the light is all" (1876, 216) Enlightening conversations, illuminating information, visions, insights—if we see, then there must be a source of light. And we do, even with our eyes closed, dreaming and daydreaming such vivid pictures without any actual light pouring through our senses. "Light is invisible, yet it allows us to see," wrote philosopher Gregory Sams, adding, "Light gives substance and form to the vegetable world, yet itself has no physical property or structure" (2009, 119).

Might light give direct, unbrokered, uncompromised sustenance to the animal world one day? Possibly. After all, atop this third rock from the sun we are already moving through space quite literally. How are we not miniature celestial bodies in our own right? All of this talk of living off light is hardly that far-fetched when you consider the basic fact that we are ourselves nothing but metabolic remnants of the sun. In *Dirt: The Ecstatic Skin of the Earth*, William Logan wrote, "Everything wants out. Everything wants to see the sun" (1995, 54). He's right. We are yearning to see the original face of our beginnings—whether from within or from without. Mastering human photosynthesis is yet another path.

Homo Solaris Needs No Tums

Like Mani, who lived almost two thousand years ago, and many others who have pondered the possibility of living off the sun, in this writing I'm merely suggesting a direction, a vector for the transhuman evolution of eating. For me personally, these are musings that flow from a place of compassion. Even as I do my best to keep my own killing and eating footprint to a realistic minimum, I remain perturbed by the lingering fact that to eat is to kill. This heterotrophic inevitability is eating at me. And it is literally eating me alive. After all, each act of consumption is a mouthful of free radicals. Food doesn't just sustain us; it also kills us. This is both a paradox and a dilemma: we have to eat food to live, and yet food kills us. It's a paradox on many levels. We have to eat to live, and yet to eat is to kill. In eating Earth, we are killing Earth and also becoming the very Earth we are killing and eating. *Homo solaris*, veritably a tree with the power of locomotion, will be hopefully free of this ethical samsara.

Breaking the Wheel of the Ourobouros

The ourobouros is an ancient symbol of a snake eating its own tail. Just like *enso*, the ourobouros is a circle. It's also a self-destructive meal-wheel, and a symbol of our samsaric condition. We are Earth eating itself, and with our modern-day appetite, as a civilization we are gobbling ourselves up. Mindful, conscious, compassionate eating and approaches like locavorism, the slow-food movement, and green technology are important, but they are only partial solutions. To break the wheel of the ourobouros for good—strategically, not just tactically—we have to figure out how to live off light. We have no option: even the sun—as a staple of light—has an expiration date. The species we eventually become will have to be green—not necessarily in pigment, but in terms of our individual metabolic pathways. The reasons are numerous: to save our fellow living beings from mindless slaughter, to save Earth from our mindless exploitation, to liberate ourselves from our heterotrophic predicament, and, in the very long term, so we don't have to tow a bunch of food-producing biodomes as we relocate to a new coordinate of space.

Beyond Eating, Beyond Money

Dostoyevsky once described money as "coined liberty" (1915, 16). Indeed, money is independence. But what is money? All money is reducible to one and the same currency: energy. That's what flows through us, what moves us, and what motivates us. Money energizes because money *is* energy. The American greenback is a symbolic leaf of life: it starts out as a banknote of photosynthesis and is metabolized time and again through the samsaric mill of metabolic reincarnations until it transmutes into a living leaf of informational and symbolic value that is redeemable for energy. Currency is literally a current—a current of energy trade. As such, money is a fundamentally heterotrophic invention. Money is an exchange of borrowed calories by those who didn't produce them in the first place. Autotrophs, the energy generators, have no need for money. Plants, unlike animals, are fundamentally and inalienably democratic and energy-independent. Each blade of grass has more sovereignty than any human nation. A blade of grass depends on nothing for its metabolic needs except abundant sun, air, water, and minerals. Each blade of grass is a dominion unto itself. It needs not ask, beg, buy, or trade. It is sovereign.

And so shall *Homo solaris* be. Reliant on the commons of sun, air, water, and minerals for physiological needs, *Homo solaris* will be beyond money and thus beyond the corruption of money and therefore fundamentally sovereign and inalienably free.

In his book *Life: A Natural History of the First Four Billion Years of Life on Earth*, Richard Fortey reminisces about the photosynthetic Eden of Precambrian time: "Cellularity had become a food chain, gobbling began, and voracity has never gone away. If there were a point in history at which Tennyson's famous phrase 'Nature, red in tooth and claw' could be said first to apply, this was it... The era of photosynthetic passivity and peaceful coexistence...had passed from the Earth, and the hierarchy of power has never subsequently been forgotten" (1998, 92–93). He's absolutely right: heterotrophy is fundamentally hierarchical. Human photosynthesis, through "techno-organic evolution," wouldn't have to mean passivity, but it certainly can mean peaceful coexistence. Human photosynthesis, as I see it, would enable each individual through possession of an independent means of energy production. A civilization of metabolically independent individuals is a natural-born democracy.

Existential Indigestion

Mind evolved out of the search for nutrition, out of the samsara of food procurement, and out of the fear of becoming food. Thus, mind is tied

in to the wheel of samsara like a bundle of empty cans to a car embla-
zoned with "Just Married." While *Homo solaris* will be beyond food,
the species won't escape existential indigestion. This wheel of mind—
the wheel of being, the wheel of existence, the wheel of sentience—
cannot be uninvented because it never really was invented. As I see it,
this inner wheel of restlessness is the conscious dimension of matter. It
isn't a separate substance as Mani thought, but a *tanha* of matter, a
built-in thirst, a built-in restlessness.

In our current incarnation as a species, we choke on food and suffer
from gastric indigestion. But even if we somehow totally unhitch ourselves from this eating carousel, we will still continue to choke on the
information that feeds our consciousness. We will continue to rumi-
nate and regurgitate the experience of life that we cannot quite swallow
and are not yet ready to digest. The meal-wheel, the wheel of information processing, the digestion cycle of our psychophysical metabolism
will continue to spin, one way or another. Life is a wheel, a cycle, a self-
sustaining circularity. As such, it has no choice but to spin, to metabolically exchange itself with its environment, to revolve around its own
axis. And while this wheel of life can be slowed down, lubricated for a
smoother spin, and retooled for better shock absorption, it will nevertheless continue rolling, as all living matter does. As long as there is
matter, there is going to be life. Matter and life, just like body and mind,
are but two words that refer to one and the same wheel of what is.

Contrary to the Buddhist canon, I personally see no problem with
this built-in existential thirst (*tanha*). This endless angst is part of the
beauty of all that is. This existential thirst and perpetual living indigestion is a source of motivation and therefore a source of change—perhaps
even the source of cosmic causality. As I see it, it is this constant seeking
that keeps the wheel of the Universe churning and spinning, revolving
and evolving. Matter has always been restless, is restless now, and, I
think, will always be restless, in some way or another. There's no need
to run from this restlessness. We *are* this restlessness. We cannot
outrun ourselves. Accept this restlessness as an essential existential
condition, a necessary precondition of our existence. If there is no
wheel, there is no life.

To Live Is to Depend

As you may recall, I opened the book with a vignette about my dad, whose favorite writing place was at the kitchen table "because the sun is really good here." Photosynthetic metabolism, like my dad's writing creativity, will, of course, remain at the mercy of light. Without light, there is no energy. So even if we, as a species, anatomically internalize photosynthesis, we will still need some supplemental form of energy when the sun is out of sight. As we pursue human photosynthesis, it is essential that we remain on some kind of flex-fuel platform, capable of both photosynthesis and, if need be, good old eating. Eating is—and will remain for centuries, if not millennia—a low-tech energy solution in the absence of sunlight.

But the larger point is that, ultimately, there is no metabolic independence in this Universe. Whatever lives depends metabolically on its environment for something. Even autotrophs aren't truly independent. Just because a plant doesn't have to kill for living doesn't mean it's truly energy independent. While self-sufficient in name, plant life depends on the sun, air, water, and minerals. Metabolic independence in any form simply isn't a cosmic option. To live is to depend. Immature dependence comes with resentment, rebellion, and mindless ingratitude. Mature dependence comes with humility, mindfulness, and grace.

Conclusion: Reinventing the Meal Reinvents the Mind

I hope this book has helped you travel someplace new in your mind. And I hope that you—and our entire civilization—will one day travel to the next level of compassion-based, minimally zero-sum, nearly autotrophic existence. I don't know about you, but it always made sense to me that humanity is not a matter of body but a matter of mind. We don't have to reinvent our bodies to reinvent ourselves as a species. We don't have to wait centuries for transhuman breakthroughs. We don't have to wait for technologically enabled human photosynthesis to begin to reinvent ourselves. By reinventing the meal psychologically, behaviorally, ethically, and spiritually, we can reinvent ourselves as a species and begin to reverse our ruinous zero-sum geopolitics.

conclusion

The Sapience of Eating

You are an amazing transmutation machine. You can take in carrots, candy bars, baked beans, bread, plums, porridge, hamburgers, or herrings—and turn them into living energy and whatever body parts you need. A carrot takes light, air, water, and earth, converting them into a crunchy, pointy, orange vegetable, and you turn this carrot into a moving, intelligent, seeing, human being. What an amazing world!

— Gregory Sams, *Sun of gOd*

The big meal-wheel has been spinning, mostly mindlessly, without much frontal-lobe supervision, for at least as long as there has been life on this planet. Our collective evolutionary history is a survival tread-mill. Life has been in the business of inventing and reinventing ever-new metabolic cycles, with life-forms finding sustenance in each others' waste, learning how to squeeze every morsel of energy out of their environment, climbing the pyramid of the solar economy through predatory competition, and also working out mutually beneficial symbiotic energy trusts.

We, the human animals, are the first species to talk about the ethics of eating our fellow life-forms. We are the first to write books about mindful eating. And we are the first to dream of energy independence (however relative it ultimately is). While we are certainly stuck in the heterotrophic cycle of zero-sum consumption, we are not stuck in a vicious cycle. Rather, as philosopher and psychologist John Dewey maintains, we can "traverse a spiral in which social customs generate consciousness of interdependencies [of cultural customs and individual habits], and this consciousness is embodied in acts which in improving the environment generate new perceptions of social ties, and so on forever" (as quoted in Sullivan 2001, 37). This book has been an attempt to do exactly that: to generate consciousness of our interdependence by way of mindful eating.

The new meal paradigm is really eating yoga in disguise. It is an attempt to reunite food, the eater, and the act of eating into a holistic whole. It is an attempt to broaden the definition of "food" to include both nourishment for the body and nurturance for the mind. It is an attempt to reduce the unnecessary overconsumption that is killing us and our fellow living beings by preloading on the fullness of breath and the fullness of the moment (that is, mind fullness). The new meal paradigm is an attempt to slow down the wheel of eating in our lives and begin to shift our existential priorities from mindless overconsumption to mindful coexperience. The new meal paradigm is a psychological reorientation that will hopefully culminate in a reinvention of the species that will free us up from our heterotrophic predicament and allow us to move beyond the corruption of money toward the autotrophic near-autonomy of *Homo solaris*.

In conclusion, consider the following image: There is a Buddhist tradition in which pilgrims travel the 2,500-mile Tea Road on foot. This pilgrimage over twenty mountain chains and across two deserts and four major rivers takes about six months. But the pilgrims don't simply walk the route; they measure the path with the lengths of their bodies. They get down and prostrate themselves forward to touch—in reverence—the ground that they traverse. Then they get up and walk up only as far as their outstretched hands reached and stop to kneel down and prostrate themselves again. In effect, the pilgrims crawl their way along more so than they walk. Dressed in body-long aprons, they work their way down the path for weeks, covering as much ground as they can in a given day in this back-breaking meditation and then bivouacking for the night. They persist through rain and sunshine, through mud and dust, through bliss and fatigue, but at all times they are spiritually in touch with the ground they traverse.

Eating is just like that. Open your mind before you open your mouth. Each bite is a kiss of reality, and each mouthful a step down this path of living. Each taste is a taste of Earth. Recognize, pilgrim of existence, that you are eating Earth and becoming Earth in one and the same eating stride. Slow down to notice the ground you walk on and the one walking, the food you are eating and the one who is eating—and see no difference.

I want to leave you with a set of four points that describe a "radical vision of the future" as envisioned by philosopher Sam Keen in his book *Fire in the Belly* (1991, 119):

1. The new human vocation is to heal the Earth.

2. We can only heal what we love.

3. We can only love what we know.

4. We can only know what we touch.

Sam Keen wasn't writing about eating when he wrote this. But he might as well have been. To eat is to know is to touch is to love is to heal this Earth that we ourselves are. Made of Earth, we are Earth. Eating, we are eating Earth and becoming Earth—hopefully, with love and self-knowledge and intimately in touch with the reality of our continuous co-creative self-transformation. That's the sapience of mindful eating! Let conscious eating be your new vocation, you, who are Earth eating Earth.

In closing, a poetic sentiment:

What's eating you, Omnivore of Consciousness?

Everything?
You've tasted all but a sense of Self?

This reality you crave
is but a subjective idea of reference.

Enlighten to your transparency:
Full of everything, you're no more than a state of hunger.

References

Altman, D. 1999. *Art of the Inner Meal: Eating as a Spiritual Path*. New York: HarperCollins.

Associated Press. 2006. Man Claims New World Record for Fasting. October 16.

Austin, J. 1999. *Zen and the Brain: Toward an Understanding of Meditation and Consciousness*. Cambridge, MA: MIT Press.

Benson, H., and W. Proctor. 2010. *Relaxation Revolution: Enhancing Your Personal Health through the Science and Genetics of Mind-Body Healing*. New York: Scribner.

Brown, S., with C. Vaughan. 2009. *Play: How It Shapes the Brain, Opens the Imagination, and Invigorates the Soul*. New York: Penguin.

Bryan, N. S., and J. Zand, with B. Gottleib. 2010. *The Nitric Oxide (NO) Solution: How to Boost the Body's Miracle Molecule to Prevent and Reverse Chronic Disease*. Austin, TX: Neogenis.

Buettner, D. 2008. The *Blue Zones: Lessons for Living Longer from the People Who've Lived the Longest*. Washington, DC: National Geographic.

Buteyko, K. P. 1977. Carbon Dioxide Theory and a New Method for Treatment and Prevention of Disease of the Respiratory System, Cardiovascular System, Nervous System, and Some Other Diseases [in Russian]. Lecture at Moscow State University, December 9, 1969, Science and life [Nayka i Zhizn], October 1977, Moscow, Russia.

Capra, F. 1997. *The Web of Life: A New Scientific Understanding of Living Systems*. New York: Anchor Books.

Center for Mindful Eating. 2011. Welcome to the Center for Mindful Eating. www.tcme.org. Accessed November 24, 2011.

Craighead, L. 2006. *The Appetite Awareness Workbook: How to Listen to Your Body and Overcome Bingeing, Overeating, and Obsession with Food.* Oakland, CA: New Harbinger.

Dadachova, E., and A. Casadevall. 2008. Ionizing Radiation: How Fungi Cope, Adapt, and Exploit with the Help of Melanin. *Current Opinion in Microbiology* 11(6):525–531.

Davis, B., and V. Melina. 2000. *Becoming Vegan: The Complete Guide to Adopting a Healthy Plant-Based Diet.* Summertown, TN: Book Publishing Company.

Davy, B. M., E. A. Dennis, A. L. Dengo, and K. P. Davy. 2008. Water Consumption Reduces Energy Intake at a Breakfast Meal in Obese Older Adults. *Journal of the American Dietetic Association* 108(7):1236–1239.

De Nicolas, A. T. 1976. *Meditations through the Rg Veda: Four-Dimensional Man.* York Beach, ME: Nicolas-Hays.

Diamond, J. 1987. The Worst Mistake in the History of the Human Race. *Discover*, May, 64–66.

Dostoyevsky, F. 1915. *The House of the Dead: A Novel in Two Parts.* New York: Macmillan.

Downer, R. 1991. *Lifesense: Our Lives through Animal Eyes.* London: BBC Books.

Dunn, R. R. 2009. *Every Living Thing: Man's Obsessive Quest to Catalog Life, from Nanobacteria to New Monkeys.* New York: HarperCollins.

Emerson, R. W. 1876. *The Works of Ralph Waldo Emerson. Vol. 1. Essays, First and Second Series.* Boston: Houghton, Osgood, and Company.

Fillmore, C. 1999. *Keep a True Lent.* Unity Village, MO: Unity School of Christianity.

Finkel, M. 2009. The Hadza. *National Geographic* 216(6):94–119.

Fortey, R. 1998. *Life: A Natural History of the First Four Billion Years of Life on Earth.* New York: Alfred A. Knopf.

Forty, S. 2003. *Symbols.* San Diego, CA: Thunder Bay Press.

Fuhrman, J. 1995. *Fasting and Eating for Health.* New York: St. Martin's.

Gandhi, M. K. 1999. *An Autobiography or the Story of My Experiments with Truth.* Ahmedabad, India: Navajivan.

Gerard, R. W. 1961. *Unresting Cells.* New York: Harper.

Haberman, D. L. 1994. *Journey through the Twelve Forests: An Encounter with Krishna.* New York: Oxford University Press.

Hirsch, A. R. 1998. *Scentsational Weight Loss*. New York: Fireside.

Hochsmann, H., and Y. Guorong (trans.). 2007. *Zhuangzi*. New York: Longman.

Ignarro, L. J. 2005. *NO More Heart Disease: How Nitric Oxide Can Prevent—Even Reverse—Heart Disease and Strokes*. New York: St. Martin's Press.

Jones, S. 1993. *The Language of Genes: Solving the Mysteries of Our Genetic Past, Present, and Future*. New York: Anchor Books.

Jung, C. 1963. *Memories, Dreams, Reflections*. New York: Pantheon.

Kabat-Zinn, J. 1990. *Full Catastrophe Living: Using the Wisdom of Your Body and Mind to Face Stress, Pain, and Illness*. New York: Delta.

Keen, S. 1991. *Fire in the Belly: On Being a Man*. New York: Bantam.

Krishnamurti, J. 1977. *Commentaries on Living: Third Series*. New York: Harper.

Krishnamurti, J. 2006. *Commentaries on Living: First Series*. Wheaton, IL: Theosophical Publishing House.

Kurlansky, M. 2002. *Salt: A World History*. New York: Penguin Books.

La Barre, W. 1954. *The Human Animal*. Chicago: University of Chicago Press.

Lawrie, A. 1998. Eating Glass. *Granta* 62:239–247.

Levy, J. 2004. *Universe in Your Pocket: 3,999 Essential Facts*. New York: Barnes & Noble.

Logan, W. B. 1995. *Dirt: The Ecstatic Skin of the Earth*. New York: Riverhead Books.

Margulis, L., and D. Sagan. 1995. *What Is Life?* Berkeley: University of California Press.

Margulis, L., and D. Sagan. 2001. Sentient Symphony. In *The Nature of Life: Readings in Biology*. Chicago: Great Books Foundation.

Margulis, L., and D. Sagan. 2002. *Acquiring Genomes: A Theory of the Origin of Species*. New York: Basic Books.

Margulis, L., and D. Sagan. 2007. *Dazzle Gradually: Reflections on the Nature of Nature*. White River Junction, VT: Sciencewriters Books.

McGlothin, P., and M. Averill. 2008. *The CR Way: Using the Secrets of Calorie Restriction for a Longer, Healthier Life*. New York: HarperCollins.

Ming-Dao, Deng. 1992. *365 Tao: Daily Meditations*. New York: HarperOne.

Moussaieff Masson, J. 2009. *The Face on Your Plate: The Truth about Food.* New York: W. W. Norton.

Nhat Hanh, T. 1993. *The Blooming of a Lotus: Guided Meditations for Achieving the Miracle of Mindfulness.* Boston: Beacon Press.

Nilsson, L. 1990. *A Child Is Born.* New York: Dell.

Norbu, C. 2006. *Dzogchen Teachings.* Ithaca, NY: Snow Lion.

Radhakrishnan, S., and C. A. Moore (eds.). 1973. *A Source Book in Indian Philosophy.* Princeton, NJ: Princeton University Press.

Ramanujan, A. K. (trans.). 1973. *Speaking of Siva.* New York: Penguin.

Reader's Digest. 2002. *The Stomach and Digestive System.* Pleasantville, NY: Reader's Digest.

Roche, L. 2001. *Breath Taking: Lessons in Breathing.* Emmaus, PA: Rodale Press.

Sagan, D. 1990. *Biospheres: Metamorphosis of Planet Earth.* New York: Bantam Books.

Sagan, D., and L. Margulis. 1993. God, Gaia, and Biophilia. In *The Biophilia Hypothesis,* ed., S. R. Kellert and E. O. Wilson. Washington, DC: Island Press.

Sams, G. 2009. *Sun of gOd: Discover the Self-Organizing Consciousness That Underlies Everything.* San Francisco: Red Wheel/Weiser.

Sayadi, R., and J. Herskowitz. 2010. *Swallow Safely: How Swallowing Problems Threaten the Elderly and Others.* Natick, MA: Inside/Outside Press.

Schick K., and N. Toth. 1993. *Making Silent Stones Speak: Human Evolution and the Dawn of Technology.* New York: Touchstone.

Schulberg, L. 1968. *Historic India.* New York: Time-Life Books.

Science Illustrated. 2010. The Superstarvers. *Science Illustrated,* July/August, 60–66.

Sharma, H. 1993. *Freedom from Disease: How to Control Free Radicals, a Major Cause of Aging and Disease.* Toronto, ON: Veda Publishing.

Somov, P. 2010. *The Lotus Effect: Shedding Suffering and Rediscovering Your Essential Self.* Oakland, CA: New Harbinger.

Spencer, C. 1996. *The Heretic's Feast: A History of Vegetarianism.* Hanover, NH: University Press of New England.

Stewart, I. 1998. *Life's Other Secret: The New Mathematics of the Living World.* New York: John Wiley & Sons.

Sullivan, S. 2001. *Living Across and Through Skins: Transactional Bodies, Pragmatism, and Feminism.* Bloomington: Indiana University Press.

Suzuki, S. 2010. *Zen Mind, Beginner's Mind.* Boston: Shambhala.

U.S. Department of Agriculture (USDA). 2011. www.choosemyplate. gov. Accessed December 10, 2011.

Walford, R. 2000. *Beyond the 120 Year Diet: How to Double Your Vital Years.* New York: Four Walls Eight Windows.

Weil, A., and W. Rosen. 1983. *Chocolate to Morphine: Understanding Mind-Active Drugs.* Boston: Houghton Mifflin.

Weitzberg, E., and J. O. Lundberg. 2002. Humming Greatly Increases Nasal Nitric Oxide. *American Journal of Respiratory and Critical Care Medicine* 166(2):144–145.

Wilson, E. O. 1993. Biophilia and the Conservation Ethic. In *The Biophilia Hypothesis,* ed. S. R. Kellert and E. O. Wilson. Washington, DC: Island Press.

Wood, J. 2000. *The Celtic Book of Living and Dying.* San Francisco: Chronicle Books.

Woolley, C. L. 1965. *The Sumerians.* New York: Norton.

World Time News Report. 2007. Major Biological Discovery inside the Chernobyl Reactor, a Fungus That Feeds on Radiation. September 22. www.wtnrradio.com/news/story.php?story=262. Accessed December 10, 2011.

Zaehner, R. C. 1966. *Hindu Scriptures.* London: Everyman's Library.

Pavel G. Somov, PhD, is a licensed psychologist in private practice in Pittsburgh, PA. He is the author of *Eating the Moment, Present Perfect, The Smoke-Free Smoke Break,* and *The Lotus Effect.* Visit his online Mindful Eating Tracker at
www.eatingthemoment.com/mindfulness-tracker.

Foreword writer **Donald Altman, MA, LPC,** is vice president of The Center for Mindful Eating and author of *One-Minute Mindfulness* and *Meal by Meal.*

 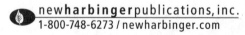